Preface:
THREE KINDS OF SIGN COMMUNICATION

The journal *Sign Language Studies* began appearing in 1972, just as signing was beginning to find a place in programs for deaf children in American schools. Signing was then accepted as one component of several in an educational philosophy called "Total Communication." When success is defined as empowering deaf children leaving school with literacy and general knowledge at or near the level attained by their hearing peers, however, the various new modes of expression and methods of instruction included under the broad label "Total Communication" have not contributed notably to success. Accepting the use of signs, at least in principle, opened classrooms to:

1. The natural language of the adult deaf community, American Sign Language (ASL)—that is, classrooms were open to it in case there were teachers who knew and chose to use it;

2. Sign vocabularies, designed to represent par-ticular elements of spoken English so accurately and completely that young deaf children addressed in these signs would automatically gain English language competence;

3. An interlanguage (also variously labeled, see below) that has grown up wherever deaf and hearing people are in constant contact.

The natural language of the adult deaf community in the United States and Canada, ASL, has never been given a chance to prove itself in education. Several reasons have been offered to explain why it has not been used as a medium of instruction. First, there are persons (both deaf and hearing) with influence in schools and in governmental agencies that fund and set standards for schools—and these persons in power will not yet admit that ASL is a language. From ignorance or out of prejudice, either unexamined or aggressively held, some of them believe that the signing of deaf people is a feeble attempt, foredoomed to failure, to represent a spoken language. They may argue also that "those deaf," who have rejected oral education cannot fully understand English. Others among them, consciously or not, desperately fear to concede that deaf people have a language of their own (and a culture and a right to be deaf and to resist attempts to make them into second-rate imitations of hearing people); for such a concession would seriously endanger their own system of beliefs and even, in many cases, their livelihood.

A second reason ASL has not yet become widely used as an instructional medium   is sheer numbers: too few hearing teachers are comfortable with it as a working second language, and too few deaf persons with ASL competence have passed the gatekeepers of education and attained full teaching status. School authorities, not having on board personnel able to teach in ASL, have naturally not authorized its use in the classrooms.

SIMULTANEOUS COMMUNICATION, AMERICAN SIGN LANGUAGE & OTHER CLASSROOM MODES USING SIGNS

Table of Contents

HV
2474
.S59
1992

1 5 8 5 5 2

may 1993

ISBN 0-932130-13-5

But a subtler reason ASL has been kept out of classrooms may be its long tradition as an "in-group" language. While even highly educated users of ASL are aware that the most skillful interpreters know ASL well, as may a few other hearing persons, these deaf "keepers of the language" still tend to use it only among themselves and avoid its use when hearing persons are not present. Many of them hold the opinion that ASL, while perfectly well suited to the needs of its users within the community, is not an appropriate language for formal education. These deaf people prefer a kind of signing that comes nearer to representing pedagogical English as used by a (hearing or deaf) teacher; in an interpreted exchange, they prefer to have the interpreter stay close to English structure and not translate from (formal) English into (intimate) ASL.

A **second class** of signing has gained wide acceptance in schools and classrooms for the deaf, as surveys of educational practice show. The one most widely used is *Signing Exact English* (SEE$_2$), but there are schools that swear by *Seeing Essential English* (SEE$_1$), others that use *signed English*™, and still others that "roll their own."

One reason for the popularity of sign vocabularies of this kind for representing English may be the ease of learning to use them. Like the pocket calculators that display a word of Language Y when a word of Language X is keyed in, these invented systems allow hearing parents and teachers simply to store in their memory a sign for each word they want to use.

All of these invented ways of representing English by prescribing a signs for a word (or an ending) make promise openly or by implication that those hearing persons who use one of these sign-word systems does not need to learn how deaf people really communicate. The promise is that with one language, English, and use of this or that particular code for its words or morphemes or suffixes, everything that needs doing can be done. Designed to make English so visible that deaf children will acquire competence in English, these codes have certainly not performed as promised. But how could they? They are neither English nor a natural sign language.

The third kind of signing also has multiple names, but unlike the consciously designed systems, it develops, without needing to be invented, wherever deaf and hearing persons interact. The common name for this kind of signing is "simultaneous communication" (also SimCom, simcom, or S/C), but it has been called "Pidgin Sign English." It is also what some people refer to when they talk of "Total Communication." It has been compared to "foreigner talk" and "learner's language," and been referred to as "sign supported speech," "a contact variety," "English signing," and otherwise.

The diversity of its names, however, does not begin to describe the variety of behavior making up this third kind of signing, which in all likelihood is really two two kinds; for it differs according to whether the person signing is deaf and knows English more or less well, or is hearing and has a less or greater competence in ASL.

This third kind of signing may be accompanied by speech or speech–like mouth movement. Hearing people may be more likely to use voice, deaf people more likely to mouth the words silently, but the practice varies in this respect as well. (The second kind of signing, of course, is expected to be used regularly along with speaking.)

Both the second and third kinds of signing, with all their variety in name and nature, and with their opponents and their advocates, have spun off controversies within the whole controversial matter of how teachers ought to teach and communicate with deaf students—in every setting from preschool to college and university. The debate on ways and kinds of signing has unfortunately often shown more emotion than thought, more of what people want to believe than what they can demonstrate.

Extreme positions have been hotly defended. Some would abolish the second and third kind of signing altogether, to leave only "pure" ASL as one language, with written, printed, or fingerspelled English as the second language in a bilingual program. Others are willing to accept simultaneous signing and speaking, and proudly point to their own and to others' educational success, which may have been gained through its use.

The theme of this monograph (in substance a republication of *Sign Language Studies* 69) is that this third kind of communication, simultaneous signing and speaking, happens in fact to be widely used in deaf education, and has been so used for generations. Before it is swept away on a tide of rhetoric, it deserves impartial and empirical study. Fortunately, some of the aspects of this kind of face–to–face communication have been carefully studied; these studies provide the theme and three major studies presented here.

This monograph is by no means directed only to researchers or teachers of the deaf or to those who set educational policy. The authors here present information of vital interest to thoughtful parents of deaf children and to deaf persons looking back on their own schooling and thinking about what might have been done better and could be done better in future.

By the time a hearing child is being addressed by teachers in school, that child has been addressed by parents and siblings and other people informally for several years in spoken language. That hearing child has also been responding with the words and intonations of the language in use for almost as long—subtract a year or so. With a deaf child in a hearing family, the case is quite different.

What the writers here suggest, plead for, or insist upon is that those others use signed language to address the deaf child *as soon as the deafness is discovered*, both at home in the preschool years and later formally in school. Only thus will the deaf child have anything like the environment of a hearing child. The writers' opinions, like those of many others, differ (a) on the kind of signing to be used at first, (b) on whether another kind of signing might be more appropriate when the deaf student enters high school and college, and (c) on whether different varieties and modes of communicating may be appropriate in different parts of the young deaf child's environment.

One document has had much to do with stirring up the current lively examination of languages and modes used in teaching deaf children. Widely circulated and discussed, it has also been a major or minor impetus to several of the writers in this issue. That document, "Unlocking the Curriculum: Principles for Achieving Access in Deaf Education", by Robert E. Johnson, Scott Liddell, and Carol Erting, is not reprinted here, but

Robert C. Johnson, editor of the newsletter *Research at Gallaudet* and other publications of the Gallaudet Research Institute, presents a first hand report of the circumstances surrounding its first publication and summarizes some of the platform and written responses to the paper. One of these not previously published appears in this issue:

Debra VanBinsbergen, who teaches deaf children in Eau Claire, Wisconsin, presents one teacher's response to "Unlocking." Accepting its main argument, she addresses some of the immediate problems that confront any attempt at implementing an ASL–based bilingual approach to educating young deaf children, problems that teachers, school authorities, and parents—not just linguists—will need to consider carefully.

Madeline Maxwell, of the University of Texas at Austin, shows that the whole matter of classroom communication—languages. modes of expression used, and rules for their use—requires the examination of cultural, linguistic, physiological, sociopolitical, and other issues. She judicially reviews an impressive amount of the published research on these issues and reaches the conclusion that we need more information, and better information, information gained from data–based research on all of these issues, before we can recommend any method with confidence.

William Newell and his colleagues, at the National Technical Institute for the Deaf, use focus groups to examine communication of the second and third kind. Their method of carefully eliciting the opinions of deaf people on these controversial topics has an obvious advantage over 'yes' and 'no' answers to the kind of survey questions more often used. The deaf adults in these focus groups are engaged in educational and related professions, and they have things well worth close attention to say about the combination of English and signs that others use in communicating with them.

Dennis Cokely (President of Sign Media and Linstok Press and a past-president of the Registry of Interpreters for the Deaf) reports on an experiment in which teachers presented to three similar groups of deaf students the same information in three ways: teacher signing only, interpreter signing as teacher speaks, and teacher simultaneously signing and speaking. Test scores on the information the students received did not show that any of the three was significantly superior to the others. (It would be unrealistic to expect that the nature of communication, of language, and of student comprehension could be explained in the same clear cut manner as, for instance, that used by recent Nobel laureates in proving the existence of quarks.) In this experiment, all three ways worked, which does not bear out the current clamor for immediately abandoning one or the other.

This monograph and the special issue of SLS of which it is a revision are made possible by the unusual commitment of the writers, and by the generous assistance of the Gallaudet Research Institute, its Editor, Robert C. Johnson, and the Dean of Graduate Studies & Research, Michael A. Karchmer. The idea of an issue examining class-room communication in context was conceived by David Armstrong, Reviews Editor, after reading several of the independently submitted articles.

WCS

1. Publication and Early Aftermath of *Unlocking the Curriculum*

Robert Clover Johnson

A manuscript arrives

In November of 1988, roughly eight months after the Deaf President Now movement brought about a profound and apparently lasting change at Gallaudet University, I was asked, as the Research Editor for the Gallaudet Research Institute (GRI), to help prepare for publication a manuscript that recommended sweeping cnanges in the communication practices used in America's deaf education programs. The manuscript, with the working title, "Language in Deaf Education," had been submitted to the GRI by three researchers, two primarily affiliated with Gallaudet's Department of Linguistics and Interpreting (Robert E. Johnson and Scott K. Liddell) and one with the GRI's Culture and Communication Studies Program (Carol J. Erting). In essence, the manuscript stated that to improve deaf students' low average academic achievement levels, classroom instruction should be conducted primarily in a natural sign language (ASL in the US) rather than in a spoken language—whether or not that spoken language is accompanied by a manual code.

My first reactions to the manuscript could perhaps best be characterized as surprise coupled with excitement. I had previously worked with Erting, having written some articles describing her research, so I was not surprised to find her here describing the benefits of fluent ASL communication with deaf students. In much of her previous writing, Erting had characterized simultaneous communication ("Sign Supported Speech," SSS in the new manuscript) as a practice that not only limited the fluency and understandability of teachers' signing, but also tended to place serious constraints on teachers' ability to understand their own students' signing. What was surprising to me in the new manuscript was not the view that ASL is preferable to SSS so much as the implicit message that circumstances could be created in which sufficient numbers of hearing teachers could be expected to learn ASL and use it fluently to teach their classes.

In Erting's earlier work it had seemed, in part at least, that the situations she observed and described in schools were not only results of school communication policies, but also, of the identities of the adult communicators—either deaf or hearing—in the classroom. The use of ASL was characterized as "symbolic" of membership in the Deaf Community and use of manually encoded English (MCE) as "symbolic" of membership in the hearing/speaking world. Erting had also described deaf people's basic challenge in life as the struggle to integrate within themselves the competing forces of their own mixed allegiances to the hearing and deaf world:

This basic contradiction between the deaf individual's social identity, constructed, in part, out of the need for community with others who share fundamentally similar experiences and can communicate them, and the deaf individual's personal identity, resulting, in part, from the physical and emotional bonds between parents and children, very often manifests itself as ambivalence toward both deaf society and hearing society. The challenge to integrate these two identities and resolve the tension these competing and conflicting categories and their symbols generate is perhaps the greatest and most constant challenge faced by the deaf individual. (Erting 1983)

Having internalized the above complex picture as my own way of understanding deaf people's life struggle, I was surprised to find that in this new manuscript the identities of teachers—either deaf or hearing—seemed almost irrelevant. It now seemed that the struggle deaf people typically face in trying to communicate with and learn from hearing teachers and parents could be practically eliminated by the full-scale implementation of more enlightened policies that would ensure that teachers and parents of deaf children—whether or not they are hearing or deaf—would become sufficiently fluent in ASL to communi-cate effectively with these children.

Although I recall feeling somewhat puzzled by this bold, new analysis of deaf students' situations, I had learned from the recent Deaf President Now movement that some of the problems that vex deaf people can indeed be changed if deaf people unite and insist that change must happen. It occurred to me that perhaps the social and linguistic geography of deaf education that I had learned as a Gallaudet new–hire in 1983 had changed significantly in six years in ways I simply did not understand. To better get my bearings on this new manuscript, I remember asking the authors certain questions on an individual basis. First, I asked Erting, "Why is it that the issue of ambivalence isn't dealt with in the manuscript? Was it overridden by the communication issue?" Erting's reply, as I recall, was, "Well, that's still there [the ambivalence issue], but the language issue is more important *now* [my emphasis]." Second, I asked Johnson, "Is this manuscript connected, somehow, to Deaf President Now?" His answer was, "It **is** Deaf President Now."

I recall asking Johnson on a separate occasion, "Do you really think sufficient numbers of hearing teachers could be prepared to teach deaf kids proficiently in ASL?" He answered, "Well, we've developed better ways of teaching ASL in recent years, for one thing, and there are already lots more hearing people who know ASL than used to be the case." When I asked Liddell the same question, he said, "Something on the order of what is done in preparation for going abroad in the diplomatic corps would work, I think. In those cases, individuals go through a nine months long immersion program before going to the country where the language is used. Hearing teachers learning ASL would certainly need at least that much."

The connection between the manuscript that soon became *Unlocking the Curriculum: Principles for Achieving Access in Deaf Education* (R. E. Johnson et al. 1989) and the "Deaf President Now" movement was later made more explicit by Liddell in a formal presentation:

> I'm going to begin with a brief description of some recent events which have led us to produce this paper. First, we've all regarded deaf education as a closed system. Parents of deaf children, deaf people themselves, and professionals in linguistics and psychology have written about the inadequacies of deaf education, but have been relatively powerless in terms of having any real influence. Then, almost exactly a year ago, deaf people rose up and took control of the premier deaf institution in the world. This event by itself raised expectations that the system might be subject to change. (in R. C. Johnson 1990)

As I played my role as an editor of this manuscript, in other words, I found myself (along with the authors, so it seemed) having to rethink some of my preconceptions, or misconceptions, about what is or is not an inevitable problem for a deaf person. I began to see this manuscript as a description of a feasible Utopia ("Well, why not?" I asked myself), in which an enlightened society removes the communication barriers that have forever bothered deaf people both at home and in school.

Although I was fully persuaded by most of the manuscript's assertions, I do recall having some trouble with two points that I felt a need to discuss in a meeting with Liddell. First, I expressed confusion over the manuscript's statement that hard of hearing as well as profoundly deaf students would best be served in classrooms in which instruction is conducted in ASL. Liddell explained that since ASL can communicate as much information in a visual channel as spoken English can through an auditory channel, then anyone with any degree of hearing trouble who can see clearly would be best advised to learn through ASL. Since my role in this situation was that of an editor (I am not a linguist or researcher of any kind) I did not endeavor to argue this point, except to speculate that lay persons might wonder if "speaking up" [talking loudly for the hard of hearing] could also work in many cases, and that this skill would be much easier for hearing teachers and parents to learn than ASL.

On this same occasion, I sought reassurance that Liddell and his co-authors would be willing to stand behind the manuscript's claim that effective use of ASL would significantly raise deaf students' average achievement levels in school. Liddell responded that "we believe this proposed program would bring deaf students' achievement levels right up to grade level." When I asked what this belief was based on, Liddell reminded me of what he had just said: "ASL can communicate as much information in a visual channel as spoken English can through an auditory channel."

Prior to this experience, I had never had occasion to work closely or extensively with Johnson and Liddell, but I knew they were both highly regarded for their work in the field of sign language linguistics. My own professional background as a writer and editor with no formal training in linguistics was so different from theirs that I at first felt it would be inappropriate for me to make substantive criticisms of the content of their manuscript. I was presently surprised, however, to discover the extent to which they valued my questions and insights and were eager to respond to my and other people's suggestions.

This account would be incomplete if I did not also mention that, as an editor, it was particularly enjoyable for me to work on a manuscript written in such a clear and direct style. I don't recall having to labor over a single sentence to help clarify its meaning. It was apparent to me from the outset that *Unlocking the Curriculum* was going to be understandable to a broad audience and was going to have impact.

Having previously written an article about a 1985 nationwide survey of teachers' classroom communication practices (1986), I was aware that in all probability, as Gallaudet's Print Shop moved ahead in January of 1989 with the first printing of *Unlocking the Curriculum* (4,000 copies), only a handful of programs in the US openly advocated use of ASL for instructional purposes, and that teachers who reported they used ASL often belied this self–report by indicating that they generally spoke or mouthed English words as they signed, a giveaway that, like most teachers of deaf students, they used simultaneous communication. It seemed quite likely to me, therefore, that if the manuscript the Gallaudet Research Institute was printing as *GRI Working Paper 89-3* were taken as seriously as I thought it deserved, it would generate considerable discussion in the field of deaf education.

With the dual motivation of preparing readers for a shock and announcing the existence of *Unlocking the Curriculum* as a publication readers might want to be aware of and possibly purchase, I composed the following summary for publication in the GRI newsletter, *Research at Gallaudet* (Winter 1989). Later, in varying forms, the same summary reappeared in *Perspectives for Teachers of the Hearing Impaired, Endeavor* (which the American Society for Deaf Children mails to parents of deaf children), and *Gallaudet Today* (for Gallaudet alumni). I present this slightly condensed version of that summary here as a review of some of the main points articulated in *Unlocking*, particularly for the benefit of any readers of *SLS* who might not have read the paper.

During the last twenty years, the total communication philosophy has been officially adopted by the majority of deaf education programs in the United States. Consequently, most teachers of deaf students now use signs in the classroom, a development widely regarded as having made classroom instruction fully accessible to deaf people. Three researchers at Gallaudet University, however, recently published a paper arguing that the nearly universal practice in total communication programs of signing and speaking at the same time (often called simultaneous communication or "simcom") forces teachers to use signs in a way that is very difficult for most deaf students to understand.

The paper, called *Unlocking the Curriculum: Principles for Achieving Access in Deaf Education*, begins with the provocative sentence, "The education of deaf students in the United States is not as it should be." The authors then proceed to cite various studies showing that deaf students, on average, continue to lag far behind hearing children in every area of academic achievement. The average reading level of deaf high school graduates, the authors say, remains at roughly the third or fourth grade, and the average performance on mathematics computation is below the seventh grade level. Comparisons of assessment data gathered over many years, according to the authors, suggest that neither total communication nor mainstreaming have significantly improved these averages.

The authors then introduce the paper's fundamental premise: that a higher rate of success could be attained if there were changes in the way deaf children are educated—changes that reflect what the authors contend is these children's need for early competence in a visually accessible, "natural" language (such as ASL) and for classroom instruction that uses that language to ensure deaf students' access to curricular material. The paper maintains, in other words, that the low academic achievement levels attained by most deaf students are not results of learning deficits inherently associated with deafness but of problems in the communication practices of the students' teachers.

The less than 10 percent of deaf students who have deaf parents already tend to achieve at higher levels in all areas (including English) than do deaf children with hearing parents. The paper states that the reason for these higher achievement levels is probably that most deaf children with deaf parents have access from birth to a natural sign language, thus giving them a strong language base during a critical developmental stage. The authors define a sign language such as ASL as "natural" because it evolved through use over a long period of time, has its own unique grammar and syntax, and was not artificially designed in an effort to represent a spoken language such as English. Through family interaction, deaf children of deaf parents generally receive early linguistic, intellectual, and social-emotional stimulation in a natural sign language that enables them to arrive in school ready to learn, with a large fund of information about the world.

The authors state that there is reason to believe that deaf children with deaf parents tend to outperform their deaf peers in spite of rather than because of America's educational system. They base this view on the fact that none of the communication policies generally maintained by schools—including oral approaches, simultaneous communication, manually encoded English, or Cued Speech—enable teachers either to fully understand children who use ASL or use ASL themselves for instructional purposes.

The paper states that although deaf children with deaf parents are thereby placed at a distinct disadvantage in school in comparison with most hearing children (who are taught in their native language) they are nevertheless far better prepared socially, linguistically, and intellectually for existing school programs than the ninety–plus percent of deaf children with two hearing parents. That majority of deaf students, the paper says, generally arrive in school with severely circumscribed funds of information about the world and poorly developed language skills in *both* spoken English and sign language.

The paper asserts that traditional communication practices used to teach deaf children in the US fail to educate deaf children because they are based on spoken English, a language deaf children cannot hear. The authors say that teachers using simultaneous communication tend to "monitor their own speech" and present sequences of signs perceived by deaf students as "bits of sentences with no obvious grammatical organization." They describe all simultaneous communication systems as "Sign Supported Speech"

(SSS) and demonstrate how the effort to speak and sign at the same time often contributes to a breakdown in the intelligibility of the signed message, making it fail to represent English, ASL, or any other language.

In the paper, the authors analyze a segment of a videotape of a preschool teacher communicating with a four–year–old deaf child. They present a transcript of the teacher's speech juxtaposed with a gloss of the teacher's simultaneous signs, then note:

The teacher consistently misarticulates signs, a problem compounded by the fact that her misarticulations often result in signs that actually mean something else; e.g. DEVIL and HORSE for RABBIT, CAN'T for CAN, and FREEZE for WANT. But more problematic is the incongruity of her signs with her spoken English. It is clear that her signing is not in any sense an exact representation of English speech. Many English words are not represented by signs, and there is no consistent pattern to what is eliminated. The end result is signed sentences that are mostly incomprehensible, often contradictory to the intended meaning, and largely incomplete.

The authors contend, in fact, that there is no conclusive evidence that deaf students actually learn English grammar from observing a manual representation of that language, even when teachers are much more proficient at articulating signs and presenting signed representations of all aspects of a spoken communication than the teacher described above. They cite a study (Supalla 1986) of the signing of deaf students who had been in a signed English environment for several years without any intervening influence from users of ASL (a situation that is quite rare). They say the researcher in that study found that each child in this "ideal" signed English setting formed an idiosyncratic grammar, containing innovations quite unlike English. "This study," the authors say, "clearly suggests that it is unrealistic to expect that exposure to signed English will lead naturally to the acquisition of competent English grammar, either spoken or signed."

The authors of *Unlocking the Curriculum* contend that the widely held belief of parents and educators that deaf children should be addressed in spoken and/or signed English in their early years and introduced to ASL much later (if at all) is the reverse of what is needed to ensure these children's optimal intellectual development, including the development of their facility in reading and writing in English. They cite studies by developmental psychologists indicating that a child's first language can and should be learned in the first few years of life and linguistic studies showing that the visual accessibility of a natural sign language such as ASL makes that language the logical first language of deaf children in the United States.

The authors go on to say that "early acquisition of ASL may also be important to our goal of teaching English to deaf children. Research on bilingualism suggests that children and second language learners need a foundation in one natural language before attempting to learn a second language." They cite one linguistic study in which it is stated that "mother tongue development facilitates the learning of the second language, and there are serious implications that without such development neither language may be learned well, resulting in semilingualism."

The authors cite and concur with statements in the report of the recent Commission on Education of the Deaf to the effect that ASL is a "full–fledged native minority language to which all of the provisions of the Bilingual Education Act should apply." Since most deaf children have hearing parents, however, the proficiency levels of deaf children in their "minority language" will naturally differ from those of children from other minority groups. Radical changes in early intervention programs and ways of advising and assisting parents of deaf children would clearly need to be adopted before teachers would be able to assume that most deaf students entering school are fluent users of ASL ready to be instructed in that language. With this in mind, the authors also quote the Commission's statement that "too seldom recognized is the need for a deaf child to have other deaf children as part of his or her peer group, and to be exposed to deaf adults." Later in the paper, the authors recommend that day care by deaf day care providers would be one way to help deaf children of hearing parents learn ASL.

The authors state that if they are correct in concluding that educational content could be taught to deaf children as effectively in ASL as it is or can be to hearing children in English, then it must follow that training programs in deaf education need to be radically changed. At present, they say, in most such programs it is rare to have a course about deaf people interacting with each other, a course that teaches about the role of ASL in the ordinary development of deaf children, or even a course that teaches a future teacher to understand or produce ASL. In fact, virtually all such programs teach only some system for Sign Supported Speech, and usually require only two or three such classes.

The authors conclude that current practices in deaf education are perpetuated, in part by the widespread belief that low academic achievement is an inevitable consequence of deafness and that the present system, which does not require that teachers learn or use ASL, is as effective as any that can be devised. "The system," according to the authors, "has been able to convince its own members and the general public that the failure of speech–centered deaf education [which the authors emphasize *includes* total communication programs] has been the fault of the students rather than of the system or the practices of the people in it." The authors maintain that if deaf children were introduced to ASL early and if teachers became proficient at using ASL to teach deaf students, the students' average achievement levels would very likely rise to levels similar to those of hearing children.

In the remainder of *Unlocking the Curriculum* the authors describe in some detail a proposed model program that, if developed, could help demonstrate the results of a system of deaf education that would use ASL for classroom instruction and that would teach English as a separate, second language. This program would e<tend from day care and preschool components through high school. The authors, who readily admit that the implementation of such a program would be a very difficult task, say that they "do not expect that such a program will quickly or easily alleviate the ills of deaf education, or that it will make the process simple or non-controversial. If there is one lesson that arises from the history of deaf education, it is that solutions to problems are quite complex. We do believe, however, that [our proposed model] will achieve much more acceptable results than any of the options currently being employed in the United States.

The following "Guiding Principles" from *Unlocking the Curriculum* suggest the model's underlying philosophy, as well as the philosophical position of the authors:

1. Deaf children will learn if given access to the things we want them to learn.

2. The first language of deaf children should be a natural sign language (ASL).

3. The acquisition of a natural sign language should begin as early as possible in order to take advantage of critical period effects.

4. The best models for natural sign language acquisition, the development of a social identity, and the enhancement of self-esteem for deaf children are deaf signers who use the language proficiently.

5. The natural sign language acquired by a deaf child provides the best access to educational content.

6. Sign language and spoken language are not the same and must be kept separate both in use and in the curriculum.

7. The learning of a spoken language (English) for a deaf person is a process of learning a second language through literacy (reading and writing).

8. Speech should not be employed as the primary vehicle for the learning of a spoken language for deaf children.

9. The development of speech–related skills must be accomplished through a program that has available a variety of approaches, each designed for a specific combination of etiology and severity of hearing loss.

10. Deaf children are not seen as "defective models" of normally hearing children.

11. We concur with one of the observations of the report of the Commission on Education of the Deaf, that "there is nothing wrong with being deaf."

12. The "Least Restrictive Environment" for deaf children is one in which they may acquire a natural

sign language and through that language achieve access to a spoken language and the content of the school curriculum.

A seminar

In January and February of 1989 the authors of *Unlocking* and the small group of GRI staff that developed the manuscript into *GRI Working Paper 89-3* experienced increasing suspense over reactions the manuscript was likely to elicit from educators, deafness researchers, parents, and members of the deaf community. This feeling was intensified by reports in Gallaudet's student newspaper, *The Buff and Blue*, that students at Gallaudet, in Nova Scotia, and elsewhere were openly expressing discontent with the sign communication skills of many of their teachers. These reports inspired some concern that *Unlocking* might channel student unrest into a revolutionary attitude reminiscent of the Deaf President Now movement, a possible consequence that gave us all—in varying degrees—a mixed feeling of uneasiness, excitement, and responsibility.

I recall participating in several meetings in January in which the authors and my supervisor, Michael A. Karchmer, Dean of Graduate Studies and Research, sought to select persons the GRI should invite to a seminar in which *Unlocking* would serve as a catalyst for discussion. There was unanimous agreement in those meetings with Karchmer's view that publishing

Unlocking gave the GRI a responsibility for encouraging and facilitating the expression of conflicting viewpoints. The effort to choose panelists for a balanced debate was hastened when an opportunity arose for the GRI to sponsor a seminar on "communication issues" to be held at Gallaudet on February 21, 1989—much sooner than any of us had anticipated. To prepare panelists for this event, to be called "Access: Language in Deaf Education," it would be necessary to put copies of *Unlocking* in the mail as soon as they left the Print Shop early in February.

David Denton, Superintendent of the Maryland School for the Deaf since 1967, was chosen to be one of the panelists because of his early and sustained leadership in promoting the total communication philosophy, which has come to be associated with the practice of simultaneous communication (i.e. SSS). Gerilee Gustason, one of the creators of SEE2, was selected to represent the perspective of those who had long advocated the use of borrowed or invented signs intended to represent English manually. Carol Padden, well known for her studies of deaf culture and the experimental use of ASL for instructional purposes, was chosen to represent a perspective more likely to favor the paper's overall goals and to offer advice concerning its possible implementation. David Martin, Dean of Gallaudet's School of Education and Human Services, was selected because of his position directing a program designed to prepare future teachers of deaf children.

Roberta Thomas, then Executive Director of the American Society for Deaf Children, was selected to represent the interests and concerns of hearing parents of deaf children.

By the time the seminar was held—in the auditorium of Gallaudet's Model Secondary School for the Deaf, on a cold, drizzly Tuesday afternoon—copies of *Unlocking* had been widely distributed and read by large numbers of faculty, students, and staff on campus and mailed or hand–delivered to a few individuals (including the panelists, of course) here and there around the US. This event marked the first occasion I know of in which the specific arguments presented in *Unlocking* were formally discussed. The interest level on campus was so high that MSSD's auditorium was filled and an overflow crowd watched the event on closed–circuit TV in several campus locations. Since a transcript of the seminar has now been printed and made generally available (*GRI Occasional Paper 90-1*), I won't elaborate here on the content of the panelists' presentations, but I will comment on some aspects of the event that I found particularly striking.

Three of the five panelists—Denton, Gustason, and Martin—had been selected largely because they each seemed likely to articulate alternative views of the educational system described as "a failure" in *Unlocking the Curriculum:* simultaneous communi-cation, manually encoded English, and teacher preparation programs for deaf education. Also, it was anticipated that these individuals might dispute the claim that instruction in ASL is both easier to understand and more likely to yield satisfactory academic results than instruction in simultaneous communication. My own experience of what actually happened, however, was that I braced myself for one form or argumentation and, for the most part, was treated to another. Instead of vigorously attacking the main points of *Unlocking*, for instance, Denton des-cribed it both as a "sharp reflection of the times" and as an outline of the "next, logical step" in deaf education. Although he expressed "dread" concerning an uncertain future for teachers and parents of deaf children, he seemed to concede at the outset that a new era, in which ASL would be the preferred language for classroom instruction, might very well be about to begin.

The bulk of Denton's presentation seemed less intended to argue that simultaneous communication should be continued than to defend total communication as having been a progressive human rights movement that had ushered in the acceptance and recognition of ASL and paved the way for the proposal set forth in *Unlocking the Curriculum.*

In spite of this apparent acceptance of *Unlocking's* arguments, however, Denton's choice of words suggested that he had profoundly mixed feelings about the document. While he described *Unlocking* as "sharp" and "logical," for instance, he described his school (MSD), himself, his teaching staff, the deaf children and graduates of MSD, and their parents with words such as "heart," "soul," "anchor," "family," "membership," "reunion," and "special body." At one point, concerning arguments in *Unlocking* favoring ASL over SSS, he exclaimed, "Do we really need this?" and began to argue that the dispersal of deaf students that has resulted from PL94-142 was "more to blame than SSS" for these students' low average academic achievement levels. Denton seemed particularly concerned that *Unlocking's* emphasis on ASL would intimidate and alienate hearing parents and teachers who had been able to participate with confidence in deaf children's instruction and upbringing as a result of the comparative ease of learning SSS.

Martin, unlike Denton, who seemed to regard *Unlocking* as a signal that a new era in deaf education was on the way, seemed to regard it as an outline of an interesting experiment that might be worth investigating on a small scale. He did not attempt to argue that teachers need not learn ASL; he even indicated that he planned to institute special classes for new teachers–in–training to ensure that they acquire a good beginners' grasp of the language. He did attempt to defend current teacher–training programs on a whole, however, in which ASL is (at best) only one of many subjects, such as curriculum theory, that must be studied. Martin argued that since socioeconomic factors and strong parental involvement have been found to be highly correlated with student achievement, regardless of the communication methods used, there is no reason to assume that use of ASL would be a decisive factor in students' academic success.

Gustason stood alone that afternoon in the attempt to defend the value for instructional purposes of what the authors of *Unlocking* had labeled SSS. She immediately acknowledged that *Unlocking* had put her into a defensive posture as a creator of SEE2 by saying she felt as if she were "on the hot seat" with a "SEE label" on her chest. She dealt rather bravely, I thought, with demands from a group of deaf people in the audience that the signing interpreters—who were sitting down to let Gustason sign for herself—return to the stage. "I thought we already had interpreters going on either side," she said. Then, to the interpreters: "Come on back onto the stage, here."

Next, Gustason proceeded to accuse the authors of *Unlocking* of withholding evidence from various studies showing the effectiveness of SEE2, implying that these studies—by Luetke–Stahlman (1988) and others—were superior to the Sam Supalla study (1986) cited in *Unlocking,* because those studies looked at large numbers of SEE2 teachers, while Supalla's looked only at one. She said those studies showed that most of what the teachers spoke, they also accurately signed (in SEE2). To her, the issue was not ASL versus SEE2 or any other system so much as competence versus incompetence at signing. At the end of her talk, Gustason aimed at the same nerve Denton had hit earlier by saying that hearing parents are less likely to become fluent in ASL than in some form of MCE during their deaf children's preschool years, and she was bothered by the concept of deaf "surrogate parents" entering hearing parents' homes to teach deaf children ASL and socialize the children into the deaf community.

Carol Padden followed Gustason to the podium and immediately opened fire on Gustason's put down of Supalla's study, pointing out that Supalla was trying to find out what deaf students *learn* from competent productions of SEE2. She said Supalla found that it didn't matter if the teachers were producing SEE2 signs for nearly everything they said if the students were not learning English from the signs and could not understand much of what the teacher was saying. Padden said she supported *Unlocking's* idea of using ASL for through–the–air communication and the concept of teaching English "through literacy" rather than through manual codes. She supported the concept of having classes with two teachers, one deaf and one hearing, each bilingual in English and ASL. She expressed concern about too many deaf children finding ASL and their own cultural identity "too late" in the present system.

Thomas brought much needed laughter to a grim, exhausted audience that afternoon with her sardonic descriptions of her and her son Jesse's encounters with audiologists, counselors, and teachers involved in deaf education, whose mission in life seemed to be to convert deaf children into hearing children. For example, she described with revulsion the misguided sentimentality of an audiologist who dreamed of helping "some deaf child hear a train." She described with alarm the confession of one of Jesse's teachers that she had no idea what her students were saying when they communicated with each other in ASL. "Imagine your hearing children having a Hungarian teacher who had only studied Pidgin English for a year," Thomas said, "even for one day as a substitute."

Thomas responded to Gustason's concerns about involving deaf adults in a deaf child's preschool language development (in ASL) by saying that, for her, "Deaf people helped me feel comfortable with my deaf child and enabled me to feel close to him."

In retrospect, I now recall that some of the concerns I had vaguely felt about *Unlocking the Curriculum* before it became a publication were pushed back into my awareness by two serious comments Thomas made that afternoon. One of these was that she did *not* support the concept of having *both* a hearing and a deaf teacher in the classroom: "A deaf teacher with eight kids sounds good to me." The other was the following: Considering the large number of hearing people involved in this model, I think that the key issues of deaf identity and self–realization risk being skirted. I don't think the stigma of deafness can be uprooted unless the entire program is managed by deaf persons. Deaf education has excluded ASL because ASL has not got much that's hearing about it, and because ASL also binds together and reflects a minority culture. The use of ASL with deaf persons involved would probably result in some improve-ment in expectation and achievement, but fully educated, truly bilingual, bicultural deaf persons can best emerge from a system that has at its core autonomous, self–directing deaf persons who share a common culture and identity. [*Unlocking*], by the way, did not disagree with this; I'm simply emphasizing it (*GRI O.P. 90-1*, p. 37).

In the question–and–answer session that followed, Erting seemed to be responding, in part, to Thomas' comment when she said that if a model program were set up, efforts would be made to ensure that by its second year, deaf people would be in charge. Nevertheless, I later found myself wondering if Thomas had really been correct when she said, "The paper, by the way, did not disagree with this." *Unlocking* certainly did not *explicitly* disagree with placing a high value on deaf identity, deaf culture, and deaf control, but the paper's emphasis, the more I thought about it, seemed to be on enabling deaf children—through ASL—to compete with "hearing norms," giving deaf children equal access to "exactly the same curriculum studied by hearing children." I began to wonder if *Unlocking* itself might be another example of the obsession to make deaf children be just like hearing children, which Thomas had ridiculed in her presentation.

In the weeks that followed, news of *Unlocking's* publication and the February 21 seminar spread via the GRI newsletter *(Research at Gallaudet)*, other publications, and the ever–reliable hearing and deaf grapevines. My office, the GRI's Scientific Communications Program, became a telephone switchboard and mail room. Confusion based on the similarity of my name to one of the authors of *Unlocking* (which has become a well known joke around campus) caused us both to get large volumes of each others' mail and telephone calls regarding this publication. Deaf organizations, deaf education programs, parent groups, and hundreds of teachers, parents, and deaf adults sent in requests for from one to one hundred copies. Within a month, our initial stock of 4,000 was so depleted that we asked the Print Shop to do a second printing. Administrators from deaf education programs called to get permission to photocopy the paper for in-house distribution. Permission was usually granted; so there is now no way to determine exactly how many copies exist. I might add that the document has proved to be so compelling to linguists and educators in other countries that *Unlocking* has now (almost two years later) been translated into five languages and is being translated into five more.

The response & informed dissent.

Along with written requests for copies, an astonishing amount of mail came to the GRI in response to

Unlocking the Curriculum. There is not enough space in this article for me to describe it all. (I may approach that task at a later time.) Much of this mail was predictable. A research group favoring oral communication sent a long letter to Dean Karchmer dismissing *Unlocking* as fallacious. Several advocates of artificial sign systems sent lengthy defenses of those systems. Other researchers sent articles alternately agreeing or complaining about this or that aspect of *Unlocking*.

Many letter writers, however, including parents, teachers, audiologists, deaf Gallaudet alumni, and others, expressed astonishment at seeing their own long–held beliefs so well expressed. Some, while generally in agreement with *Unlocking*, dwelt on problems the letter writer had experienced trying to realize—without sufficient support—some of the goals outlined in *Unlocking*. I submitted one of the most eloquent of these letters—by a teacher from Eau Claire, Wisconsin named Debra Van–Binsbergen—to Bill Stokoe, and I am delighted that this letter, with its list of seemingly intractable concerns, is being reprinted here.

As a series of forums and working groups to discuss *Unlocking* were being scheduled for the spring at Gallaudet, I vented some of my frustration over this protracted affair by writing a spoof, called "Heretics Unlock Pandora's Box," for the April Fool issue of *On the Green* (a weekly Gallaudet newspaper). By April 4, when an Open Forum featuring Johnson and Liddell was held in Gallaudet's Ely Center Auditorium, I was eager to witness a new discussion of the issues. I supposed that, by then, some new arguments might be presented, so I was a bit disappointed when Liddell and Johnson were asked once again to present their arguments favoring a natural sign language over an artificial system.

In retrospect (although I could not then have articulated this), I see that I was hoping to hear some discussion of the problem hinted at in Thomas' comment about deaf culture being "skirted." I believe it was largely for that reason that I was so interested when Harry Markowicz (one of the first contributors to *SLS*, whom I had met but did not yet know well) stood up— visibly nervous—and carried on a brief exchange with Liddell that I later described in *On the Green* as follows:

Harry Markowicz, a Gallaudet English professor who has studied sociolinguistic aspects of the deaf community for many years, asked Liddell, "Can hearing people learn ASL?"

Liddell replied, "A hearing person will always have an 'accent' and will probably never achieve native fluency, but I have no doubt that with the right environment and years of effort, it is possible for hearing people to learn ASL."

Markowicz responded that, in his opinion, ASL is the language of an ethnic minority group and, as such, is never fully given or shared with hearing people. He said he believed that the most that motivated hearing teachers could hope for would be to learn a contact

variety of signing with mixed elements of English and
ASL. "Nevertheless," he added, "this variety of signing
would be far better than presently used communication
systems for teaching."

A bi-weekly series of "working groups" in Fowler
Hall followed, in which the organizers generally tried to
focus discussion on the debate between ASL and
simultaneous communication. A few students at those
meetings testified that lectures given in simultaneous
communication were difficult and often exhausting to
follow, while lectures in ASL are "easy on the eyes" and
much easier to understand. The developers of various
artificial systems representing English continued to
explain their motives and results, although I suspect
they may have felt like defendants in a Nuremberg trial.

One presenter, for instance, explained in detail how
the sign TREE, repeated to mean 'forest', was initialized
with a 'J' by the system's committee to signify 'jungle'.
This was done, the presenter said, because there was no
sign for jungle in ASL. Gil Eastman, deaf playwright,
who happened to be present, raised his hand and
showed everyone present the ASL sign JUNGLE,
suggesting that the committee must not have sought out
a sufficient number of deaf informants.

A closer view

Although the working groups were fascinating, I
began to feel that their focus on ASL versus
simultaneous communication was too narrow. After

rereading an article co-authored by Markowicz and James Woodward (1978), called "Language and the maintenance of ethnic boundaries in the deaf community," I was even more certain that the working groups might benefit from a shift of focUS I contacted Markowicz and indicated to him that my curiosity had been piqued by his comments at the Open Forum. He agreed to let me tape an interview with him concerning his views on *Unlocking*. What follows is a transcript of that interview:

Interviewer: I sensed in your comments at the Open Forum two weeks ago that you have some strong reservations about certain aspects of *Unlocking the Curriculum*, and yet, on what many people consider the paper's main topic, that is, the advantages of using a natural sign language over using simultaneous communication and manually coded English, you seem to agree with the paper. I wonder if you could explain a little bit about your points of agreement with the authors on this particular subject.

Markowicz: Yes. Well, when you listen to people signing and talking at the same time you can hear that most of them don't talk normally. There is something strange about this kind of English—at least the way most people produce it. They're speaking more slowly, for one thing, and there are other distortions in the way they're talking. In the early 70s, as I recall, Bellugi and a colleague [1972] compared the rate of speaking and signing when they are done separately by the same ASL-

English bilingual. What they found was that the production of propositions in the two languages tends to proceed at about the same rate of speed. However, twice as many English words as signs are required to express the same propositions. What does this mean? It means that on the average it takes twice as long to produce a sign as to say a word. It also means that the average sign in a signed utterance—when it does not accompany speech—contains twice as much information as the average word in a spoken utterance. If you think of ASL features such as negative incorporation and directionality, it becomes clear why this should be the case. Thus, the problem with simcom is that the rates of producing words and producing signs are so divergent that they cannot be reconciled without some modifications, such as slowing down one's speech so that it becomes distorted, and/or by dropping signs. Normally, both of these happen, so that the objective of making an exact visual representation of English, by matching up signs and words, is defeated immediately. Consequently, deaf children in a total communication setting are not exposed to a consistent matching of signs and words.

Interviewer: Gerilee Gustason seems to maintain that many teachers who learn SEE2 are able to match their spoken words with signs for about 90% or even 100% of what they speak. Now, do you find that claim incredible, or is the fact that the teacher is able to produce SEE2 signs to represent what the teacher said meaningless from the point of view of a child who can't hear the spoken English? What do you make, in other words, of this claim that teachers can represent what they say by using proficiently some form of signed English?

Markowicz: I suppose it could happen, but I doubt that it happens very frequently. What she is talking about reminds me of the "methodical signs" invented by the Abbé de l'Epée, which matched signs with French words so well that the Abbé's students were able to write in perfect French texts that he dictated to them using signs. As a *tour de force*, he even got some of the students to do this in Latin, German, Italian, and English. However, in spite of this feat, the students generally were incapable of writing a correct French sentence on their own. One reason for this is that even if one is able to reconcile the different rates of signing and speaking so that you could have a consistent one-to-one match between signs and words, the result is still lacking some of the most important linguistic information in the utterance, namely, the prosodic features. Prosodic features present utterances in meaningful chunks so there is no need for extensive a.alysis by the listener. These features, which are missing from all systems intended to represent a spoken language visually, include intonation patterns, stress, pauses, etc. The native speaker of English can process utterances lacking prosodic features, when reading written English. For the deaf student, however, the lack of prosodic features in such systems as SEE1, SEE2, LOVE, and even more natural forms of signed English, is likely to augment the difficulty of learning a language the student can't hear. Let me add here that learning English through literacy is not at all a simple matter either, for essentially the same reasons. Our writing system doesn't represent intonation patterns, most clause boundaries, etc.

Interviewer: So, in a nutshell, do you agree with statements in *Unlocking* to the effect that simultaneous communication handicaps teachers from communicating effectively with deaf children?

Markowicz: Oh, definitely. For one thing, it's not a very natural thing to do for most people. Maybe it is for hearing children of deaf parents, or some others, but for most people it is stressful. I also agree with the authors of *Unlocking* that hearing signers are more fluent and better communicators if they learn to sign without voice. I should say that I'm not against speaking and signing simultaneously in principle. In fact, there are occasions where it is both appropriate and necessary.

Interviewer: Do you agree with the authors that total communication and its usual manifestation in the classroom as simultaneous communication has been a failed experiment? Do you find any redeeming aspects to the total communication movement?

Markowicz: Okay; there are two aspects to that question. There's the school situation and there's the situation of deaf people in a hearing society. And I think that in many ways total communication has helped deaf people. It has helped them integrate better socially and economically, essentially by getting more recognition for sign language: ASL or whatever. For example, it is perfectly acceptable now to have interpreters for all kinds of situations. It has helped the growth of a movement among deaf people themselves to fight for their right to be deaf. If you compare the situation and life conditions of deaf people today to the period before total communication, 25 years or so ago, I think there have been some remarkable changes—from an outsider's point of view anyway. Now, in education, it's completely different. Total communication was intended to help deaf children academically, and especially to learn English; that was one of its main objectives. And if you look at it from that point of view, I think we know now that deaf children are not any better educated than they were before. I know that, as a teacher of English at Gallaudet, although I wasn't teaching twenty years ago, the present students in the English language Program—many of them—don't know much English, or don't know English well. This is true, although most of them were brought up during the last twenty years in some form of total communication. So, from that point of view, total communication has been a failure. As *Unlocking* points out, Annual Survey data have shown that average academic achievement levels have remained low in spite of the incorporation of signs into classroom instruction. The emphasis in total communication continued to be getting deaf people to learn to speak and learn English, but it didn't work for reasons that are clear to linguists. In fact, it was predictable that it wouldn't work.

Interviewer: *Unlocking the Curriculum* asserts that if the deaf children's teachers—and ideally their parents as well—would learn and use a natural sign language (ASL in the US), at home and in school, these children would have much greater access to learning. In fact, the document seems to put much of the blame for deaf children's low average academic achievement levels on teacher's ignorance of ASL. Do you agree with this?

Markowicz: *Unlocking the Curriculum* seems to make the claim that deaf children would be just like hearing children if they were brought up by parents and teachers who know ASL. I think that if you accept that premise, you are going to be disappointed. Using ASL presents both theoretical and practical problems. How can teachers learn ASL? More difficult is: how can parents learn ASL? Learning a foreign language requires a great amount of time and interaction with people who know the language. In this case, that would mean forming relationships with deaf people. Now, we could assume that because teachers are professional they could eventually be trained, by devoting a good part of their training to learning ASL. On the other hand, even if parents are well motivated to learn ASL, they may not have the time and energy to devote to it. They may have other children and jobs and so on. I don't think we can really expect many parents—or even professionals—to learn ASL; Americans in general don't learn foreign languages well. But that's assuming that hearing people can learn ASL. I'm not at all sure that it's desirable. Now we have to stop and clarify what we mean by ASL because if we mean by ASL what linguists have been defining as ASL it's the language deaf people use among themselves in their everyday lives and in informal interactions. Other people use ASL in a much broader way, but since the authors of *Unlocking* are linguists, I have to assume that they mean ASL the way linguists have been using the term. In that case, I think that the problem is that, being a language of what I consider to be an ethnic group, this language is not given to outsiders. The only way you can have access to it is if you are a member, or a prospective member. And you can only be a prospective member if you are a young deaf child being acculturated by others: by peers or older deaf children or in families with deaf parents or older deaf siblings. Usually this happens only in residential schools.

Generally, oppressed minority groups or ethnic groups don't give their language to outsiders. Not that they plan this out or that it's a policy, but it simply is not done. It is not done because it keeps outsiders out. It prevents people who are not members of the ethnic group from being involved. The expectation that somebody who is from outside will somehow hurt you or turn against you is always possible. Particularly, it may mean that outsiders would speak for the group. According to some people—and I agree with them—to be deaf means that others speak for you. In a literal sense, and also in a more general sense, hearing people or hard of hearing people, who have not been socialized into the deaf community, explain to others what the deaf community is or what deaf people are like.

I don't think, in spite of what some deaf militants might say, that deaf people are willing to give their language away, and there's a lot of evidence to show that they don't. Another way of seeing this was expressed by a deaf person of a deaf family who mentioned that it was embarrassing for her to see hearing people trying to sign in ASL. I think that a similar thing is felt among other groups, such as black Americans. If black Americans hear a white person speaking black English, it is not appreciated. They may think the white person is making fun of them or that some part of their being or their identity is being trespassed or stepped upon by an outsider. Being Jewish, I don't expect ever to meet a gentile who knows Yiddish; I don't mean just a few words like "chutzpah" or "schlep," but really knowing the language. If I did ever meet such a person, I would want to know, right away, how that person learned it, and secondly, I would probably not completely trust him or her.

Now, what's interesting about that is that in Israel, as regards Hebrew, which is the national language, there is no such feeling about Hebrew. It is a national language.

It is not the language of an oppressed minority group;
while Yiddish was always the language of an oppressed
minority group. And it's the same with Romany, which
is the language of Gypsies. I know, from what I've read,
that Gypsies don't share that language with outsiders.
As far as ASL is concerned I am no judge, but I have
assumed that there are certain areas of the language that
are not used with outsiders. I have been told by hearing
people who sign ASL (or something close to it)
extremely well that they have been in situations in
which they used with deaf friends some of these
expressions that are not generally shared with outsiders
and they caused an uncomfortable reaction.

It has been said that all disagreements are
disagreements about semantics. Based on comments
made during the question and answer exchange
following the first Gallaudet seminar, where *Unlocking*
was discussed, my understanding is that while its
authors advocate that teachers and parents should learn
ASL, they expect that what would actually be used is
what has been called PSE or a contact language variety
between ASL and English.

Interviewer: If there is a problem with even highly
motivated hearing teachers learning ASL and using it to
teach deaf children in the classroom, would you
advocate that deaf teachers be increasingly trained to
teach deaf students and would that be something of a
solution to many of the problems we're seeing in
achievement levels and other education problems?

Markowicz: I look at it from the opposite perspective. To me, even before I knew anything about education of the deaf, it seemed that the normal situation would be to have deaf schools, just as you have Catholic schools or Jewish schools in which most, if not all, of the teachers and the administration are Catholic or Jewish, because it is not only a matter of language but a matter of culture as well. Even if hearing people learned ASL extremely well, they still wouldn't be part of the deaf community. To be a member of any community you must be identified by the members as one of them. If hearing people could become members of the deaf community, hearing children of deaf parents would not have felt the need to create such organizations as CODA (Children of Deaf Parents). Hearing people might become knowledgeable in an abstract sense about the culture of deaf people in the way an anthropologist may know about a culture. I'm talking about culture as a way of living, as a way of seeing the world. For deaf people, that includes ways of dealing with the hearing world: knowing how to make hearing persons comfortable—in an interaction, for instance. So to your question, I would say obviously there should be deaf teachers. And I don't mean that all schools necessarily should have only deaf teachers, because I don't know that there are enough deaf people who necessarily want to go into teaching. Some schools could follow different models altogether. But I would think that there should be some schools that are deaf schools, really deaf schools with deaf teachers, and they could occasionally have hearing teachers also, but basically they would be deaf schools with deaf teachers and deaf administrators. I believe that what I've just described here is what the authors of *Unlocking* express in their guiding principles, in particular the fourth one.

Interviewer: Hearing parents always worry about their deaf children fitting into society as a whole, which is primarily populated with hearing people. Do you think that a deaf school with deaf teachers would be better equipped to prepare deaf children for the hearing world than a deaf school with primarily hearing teachers?

Markowicz: I don't know that hearing teachers can prepare deaf people for fitting into a hearing world, since they haven't had to deal with being deaf in a hearing world. I think only a deaf person can impart that kind of knowledge to deaf children, not only because of that person's own experience, but also the experience that is shared by members of the deaf community, the accumulated knowledge about the world as it is seen not only by deaf people but also knowledge about the hearing world. And only a deaf person can show them how to manage being a member of a small minority in a large hearing majority. So, in brief, I would think that they could learn more about the hearing world from deaf teachers. And I think that when deaf children leave school and begin to interact with deaf adults, that's when they learn more about the hearing world. I've observed myself the kinds of situations where a younger deaf person was being taught strategies and ways of actually doing things so that one can function better in the hearing world—with more independence and self-confidence.

Interviewer: The title of *Unlocking the Curriculum* suggests that the goal of any education is to impart to students a certain type of curriculum and it is emphasized there that the curriculum should be the same for deaf students as for hearing students. I gather from what you're saying that you feel it should be different in some respects, particularly in certain practical matters related to coping and managing about which deaf teachers could advise deaf children. But what about the core of most curricula, which would seem to include reading, writing, arithmetic, history, the English language, etc. Do you feel that deaf teachers would be the best ones to impart that kind of information, and how would the curriculum in a deaf school with deaf teachers relate to standard curricula?

Markowicz: I imagine that the curriculum would be basically the same; however, the way it is imparted to students by deaf teachers would probably make greater use of more visually oriented strategies. There would also be a lot of informal learning as a result of having deaf teachers, through their interaction with pupils. The problem is complex, because you may not have presently many deaf people who could go into the classroom and do what would work best to teach deaf children. Presumably—and this I think happens often—

what people do, no matter what they've learned in theory about how to teach and how to do things, they tend to revert to the way they were taught. In France, where bilingual education for deaf children has been an objective since the late 1970s, LSF/French instruction has been practiced in a number of schools for the last ten years. I recently visited some "bilingual" classes there in which all the teachers were deaf. No hearing people were involved in teaching. And in the class where they learned French, the materials that were used were the same as those used by hearing teachers with hearing classes. In fact, these special classes are held in a public school for hearing kids. I found it disconcerting to see that the teacher was teaching the same way that she had probably been taught French by her hearing teachers, and it didn't seem like a very effective way. So, it may be some time before there are many deaf teachers who feel free enough to devise and use their own strategies about how to approach teaching deaf children, so that they can take advantage of their visual abilities. Not that there are no such teachers. There *are* deaf teachers able to do this, but there are not enough of them at this time. That's the problem.

Interviewer: Carol Padden, in the recent seminar on *Unlocking*, mentioned that she thought all deaf adults have learned or improvised certain strategies for understanding and remembering rules about English that probably differ from the strategies that hearing people use, since their strategies are based on speech.

Do you think there may be some way that deaf people who want to be teachers could become more conscious of how they learned English and actually use those strategies for teaching English?

Markowicz: You're getting into an area where I don't want to venture. I don't know . . .

Interviewer: Okay. Do you mean this is unexplored territory and it's for deaf people themselves to figure it out?

Markowicz: Well, yes. It does seem to me that this is one of many areas where deaf people are more likely to have the best insight. But I feel I should say that the problems of deaf education are really extremely complex and may not have any ideal solutions satisfactory to everyone directly implicated: deaf children, their parents, and deaf adults.

After the interview, I urged Markowicz to try to present some of the views he'd shared with me at the next working group. We attended together, but the large group (nearly 40 people) seemed to be so intent on discussing the ASL versus simcom issue that Markowicz confined his few comments to that subject, in support of the arguments in *Unlocking*. Later, after discussing the possibility with Karchmer, who was hosting the working groups, Markowicz was offered some time in the last scheduled working group to give a brief presentation of his views concerning problems associated with simultaneous communication. I had wanted him to discuss his and Woodward's ethnic boundaries paper instead, but it occurred to me that Markowicz still might get into that subject once discussion was under way.

When that working group met in the Edward Miner Gallaudet building's Orientation Room, Markowicz articulated on stage a number of points concerning the deficiencies of simultaneous communication, then went back to his seat. Johnson thanked him for adding to the growing list of problems associated with SSS, then commented that much more extensive training in ASL is clearly needed among future teachers of deaf students.

At this point, Markowicz stood up and said, "Having agreed entirely with the authors of *Unlocking the Curriculum* on the advantages of ASL over the various artificial systems representing English, I'm sorry to have to disagree with them concerning what needs to be done about it. Although I'm in favor of hearing people learning a more natural form of signing, I'm not convinced that sufficient numbers of hearing people can learn ASL well enough to use it effectively in the classroom, and I'm not at all sure, either, that it is entirely appropriate that they do so, since this language is primarily used by deaf people among themselves."

"I disagree with you," Johnson said. "I think that's just another excuse for hearing people not to learn ASL."

Although eighteen months have passed since that brief exchange (which often comes back to mind), I cannot say that the full meaning of the subtle but important conflict between the views of Markowicz and Johnson is yet clear to me. One man seemed to be saying that although deaf children would indeed get more information if their teachers knew and used ASL, there is a kind of social taboo that will always keep ASL out of hearing people's hands, so the teachers that are most needed by deaf children are deaf teachers. The other seemed to be saying that the educational benefits that would result from fluency in ASL among teachers are so great that it would be unconscionable for hearing teachers not to join deaf teachers in the use of that language in the classroom. Who is right? I do not know.

In May of 1989 my mind at last moved away from *Unlocking the Curriculum* toward Gallaudet's next looming preoccupation, The Deaf Way Conference and Festival. Although I quickly became immersed (as did the entire Gallaudet campus) in preparations for that event (which took place in July), I did have a lengthy discussion about *Unlockingw*with James Woodward, who had been in South America for several months and who seemed perturbed by something about this new document. I reminded him that when he had been analyzing data from the 1985 communication survey conducted by the GRI's Center for Assessment and Demographic Studies (Woodward & Allen 1987), he had told me he was distressed to discover that scarcely any teachers in the US were using ASL in the classroom. I indicated to him that I would have supposed he would favor many of the proposals in *Unlocking.* "I *do*," he said. "I favor many of the goals. But what the paper is talking about, really, is a social as well as a linguistic change, and because there are so many sociolinguistic problems involved, you can't expect to change the language used in the classroom successfully overnight. There must be careful research and planning before attempting such changes."

After we discussed these social changes a bit more, I advised Woodward to write a paper explaining his concerns about *Unlocking*. "I already *have*," he said. "I wrote it back in 1978 for the Second National Symposium on Sign Language Research and Teaching, of which the theme was American Sign Language in a bilingual, bicultural context. In it I focused on the many practical problems in implementing sociolinguistic change in the educational system for deaf students. S.urprisingly, the paper is cited in *Unlocking* as being in support of the ideas there. But unfortunately *Unlocking* does not discuss any of the problems focused on in my paper (Woodward 1978)."

For me, what began as an editorial assignment two years ago became an intellectual adventure that has not yet reached a resolution. It is clear that *Unlocking* opened a much-needed discussion of communication issues that many had wrongly assumed were settled twenty years ago by "total communication." At times I have been distressed to observe how easily debate concerning *Unlocking the Curriculum* can degenerate into quarrels; but reading the other articles in this volume and discussing with colleagues various bold experiments now under way here and there in the US and abroad convinces me that much fruitful discussion still can and should occur.

References

Bellugi, U.

  1972   Studies in sign language. In *Psycholinguistics & Communication,* O'Rourke ed. Silver Spring, MD: National Assn. of the Deaf. 68-84.

Erting, C.

  [1983   Deafness, communication & social identity: An anthropological analysis of interaction among parents, teachers & deaf children in a preschool. Unpublished doctoral dissert., American University, Washington, DC.]

Johnson, R. C.

  1986   How teachers communicate with deaf students, *Perspectives for Teachers of Hearing Impaired* 4(5), 9-11.

Johnson, R. C. (Ed.)

  1990   *Access: Language in Deaf Education* (Proceedings of a Seminar Concerning "Unlocking the Curriculum: Principles for Achieving Access in Deaf Education"). *GRI Occasional Paper 90-1.* Washington: Gallaudet Research Institute.

Johnson, R. E., S. Liddell & C. Erting

  1989   Unlocking the curriculum: Principles for achieving access in Deaf education. *GRI Working Paper Series, No. 89-3.* Washington: Gallaudet Research Institute.

Leutke-Stahlman, B.

1988   SEE2 in the classroom: How well is English grammar represented? In *Signing English & TC: Exact or Not?* Gustason ed. Los Alamitos, CA: Modern Signs Press.

Markowicz, H. & J. Woodward

1978   Language and the maintenance of ethnic bound-aries in the deaf community, *Communication & Cognition*, 11(1), 29-33.

Supalla, S.

[1986   Manually coded English: The modality question in signed language development. Unpublished Masters Thesis, University of Illinois, Urbana-Champaign.]

Woodward, J.

1978   Some sociolinguistic problems in the implementation of bilingual education for deaf students. In *American Sign Language in a Bilingual-Bicultural Context*, Caccamise & Hicks eds. Silver Spring, MD: NAD. pp. 183-203.

Woodward, J. & T. Allen

1987   Classroom use of ASL by teachers, *Sign Language Studies* 54: 1-10.

Note: Markowicz & Woodward (1978) and Woodward (1978) are reprinted in Woodward, J. 1982. *How You Gonna Get to Heaven If You Can't Talk to Jesus?* Silver Spring, MD: T.J.Publishers, Inc.

ONE TEACHER'S RESPONSE
TO "UNLOCKING THE CURRICULUM"

Debra VanBinsbergen

I am a teacher of the hearing impaired, employed by a Cooperative Educational Service Agency (CESA #10), at Robbins Elementary School in Eau Claire, Wisconsin.

As a teacher of hearing impaired elementary students, I think the idea of teaching English as a second language to hearing impaired children is an excellent one. I also think teaching deaf children ASL as their first language makes sense, since then the children have a first language to build upon in order to learn English more efficiently. I have seen the advanced skills of deaf children who have deaf parents as compared to those of deaf children who have hearing parents. I agree that this discrepancy can be attributed to the firm language base the children have been building since birth, but just as important is the consistency of visual language input in their homes. I also definitely agree that ASL instruction should be a stressed part of teacher training programs, and I wish it had been in my program.

However, although I feel the proposals made in "Unlocking the Curriculum" are very good ideas, for many reasons I have concerns as to how they can be implemented. First, I would like to discuss hearing parents. Parents of a newly diagnosed deaf child have a difficult time making any sense of the onslaught of new information and jargon concerning deafness. They want to make the right choices concerning communication method and edu-cational placement. But the realities are [that] these parents cannot spend every waking minute with issues concerning their deaf child. They have other pressing concerns in their lives including jobs, other children, schedules, and just trying to keep their marriage together. (The added tensions of having a deaf child will break up many of their marriages.) Some of these parents will be doing all they can to take a sign class or two and try to use signs as consistently as they can to supplement their speech.

As a professional who does not live with the day-to-day struggles of having a deaf child, I cannot judge these parents and tell them they are not doing enough—that they must not only learn to sign but they must learn ASL, a totally different language. They must then teach this new language, one which they are not fully comfortable with, to their deaf child and to his or her siblings and to relatives and friends. Of course, having everyone signing is the ideal situation for a deaf child, but learning ASL is a much more formidable task for hearing people than learning a signed English system. My greatest fear is that these families will burn out from tremendous expectations and they will give up altogether. I have seen this happen with those trying to learn an English system and, for most, that is an easier task than learning ASL.

The help of deaf adults is often cited as the answer to some of the problems of learning ASL. From my experience, there are very few deaf adults willing to spend their time to help every parent and teacher who wants to learn ASL. Deaf adults have their own lives and they do not always appreciate hearing people interfering. "Getting involved in the deaf community" is not as easy as it sounds, especially when hearing people are generally not welcome at club gatherings or even church services. Besides, in many smaller communities, deaf adults cannot be reached within commuting distance.

In my own experience, I invited four deaf adults into my classroom throughout the last school year to share with my students Only one of the four even used ASL! The one who did was a high school senior from the state school for the deaf, and I doubt if he would be interested in running a day care [program] for deaf children, as was suggested in "Unlocking the Curriculum."

There are undoubtedly other deaf adults in my community, and I will continue to seek them out, but my point is that these people are not as readily available as has often been suggested. I can also say from experience that many hearing parents would not even consider teaching their child ASL as a first language (and I must stress, this is the parent's decision to make, not the teacher's). They would actually become angered at the suggestion. In fact, the trend now seems to be leaning toward using manual systems, considered closer to English, such as Cued Speech. Hearing parents want their child to be like them as much as possible and to participate and succeed in the hearing world. It is difficult for a parent to accept an approach that seemingly works backwards: in order to teach the deaf child English, he or she must first learn another language, namely ASL. Actually, I think some parents might support exploration of this approach, but would not be willing to jeopardize their own child's prime language acquisition years for experimentation.

Parents are also concerned for their hearing children. One parent told me her hearing daughter's first grade teacher decided the problems her daughter is having with language have been caused by the use of sign in their home. This parent was very upset that her efforts to help her deaf child could actually be hurting her other children. This family does not even use ASL, but rather simultaneous communication. I do not agree with, nor do I condone the first grade teacher's comment, but this is a fear of many parents: that they are depriving their hearing children of the opportunity to grow up normally hearing and speaking English in the home. The use of ASL, as opposed to a simultaneous system, would mean less English was being used, making this situation for the hearing siblings even worse.

As a teacher, I see many obstacles in the classroom when I think of trying to implement the proposals made in "Unlocking the Curriculum." First and foremost, how do I become skilled enough in ASL to use it in the classroom? As I mentioned before, this was not included to any great extent in my teacher training, and although I have taken many lowlevel community courses, there are no classes offered for those with more advanced skills. I have watched videotapes, and attended conferences and plays, but I do not feel well enough equipped to use ASL consistently in the classroom.

It is easy for others to lament that teachers need better training in ASL, but the truth is, the training is not available even for those who are interested in getting it.

Another obstacle I see for teachers is how other skill areas that we are expected to teach can be included in our instruction, such as auditory training, speech reading, and speech. I do feel a mastery of language is the most important goal, but these other areas also need to be addressed. Many deaf children have the potential to learn speech and speech reading, and to use their residual hearing to its greatest capacity. But since the child will be using ASL and will not be using speech in the classroom, or at home for that matter, he or she cannot be expected to make significant gains in speech when given only 20 minutes practice a day while with a speech clinician. Besides, the clinician would not get results when the child never sees a need for using speech. Also, there would be limited need for the auditory training units school districts have spent many thousands of dollars to purchase. As with language, the areas of speech, speech reading, and use of residual hearing must be developed early in a child's life or much of the potential is lost. Many parents and professionals would find it very difficult to accept this loss of potential in their deaf children.

A last obstacle I want to mention in my teaching situation is that of the varied hearing impaired students I work with. Because [the population with] hearing impairment is a low-incidence population, children with varied hearing losses and abilities are often grouped together. I have students with hearing losses ranging from mild to profound, some with multiple handicaps, and a variety of elementary ages, all grouped together (but I do not have any deaf children with deaf parents). This arrangement has some benefits: as in a one room school house, the children learn from each other and are encouraged by the successes of others. They also have a feeling of belonging to a group, which is especially important since they all move into and out of different mainstream classrooms throughout the day. The children also get a taste of the real world where one often needs to use creative communication to get ideas across to hearing persons. However, these differing communication modes are precisely what make the teaching most difficult. Actually, the students do beautifully: the hard of hearing child learns some sign, the moderate to severe[ly deaf] child benefits from being able to speak, lip read, and sign, while the profound[ly deaf] child speaks, pantomimes, or writes as necessary to communicate with others.

However, the teacher needs to use a system that everyone can understand, and simultaneous communication seems to be the answer. It is not a perfect solution, as has been pointed out in "Unlocking the Curriculum." This kind of signing while speaking creates a sequence of signs that is not as easy to understand as ASL for the deaf child. But the fact remains [that] school districts cannot provide a separate classroom environment for perhaps two deaf children who could benefit from ASL; and parents are enjoying their right to keep a child at home and in the local school instead of sending him or her to a residential school.

In conclusion, I agree with the proposals made by the authors of "Unlocking the Curriculum." I believe ASL is the easiest language for deaf people to understand and should be used to teach English as a second language. When a classroom for deaf children has been set up with parents willing and able to use ASL, with adequate training resources available to teachers and parents, with deaf and hearing teachers team–teaching, with deaf adults working as teacher's aides, and with the deaf children homogeneously grouped; then, in my opinion, the ideal will have been reached.

Unfortunately, since this is not the reality for most programs, especially small ones, we should invit deaf adults to speak to our classes and provide volunteer help. We can show videotapes featuring ASL users and use ASL in the classroom when possible, especially for teaching about deaf culture, story telling, and explaining new or difficult concepts. I also believe that English can be taught as a second language, regardless of how much they have actually used ASL. Most deaf children pick up the grammar characteristic of ASL without much exposure, simply because it comes naturally.

I heard two teachers speak at a conference (Wausau, Wisconsin, Fall, 1988) about how they have been using the ESL approach with deaf college students. I believe many of these ideas could be used to present language to deaf children who do not even have a firm language base with which to work. Because—let's face it—most young hearing impaired children are not going to become fluent in ASL, and we need some ideas to help the students we have in the classroom now. If anyone has specific suggestions as to how to implement an ESL approach with hearing impaired elementary children, or ideas to solve any of the problems I have mentioned above, I would like to hear about them.

SIMULTANEOUS COMMUNICATION: THE STATE OF THE ART & PROPOSALS FOR CHANGE

Madeline M. Maxwell

The theory & practice of simultaneous communication

It has been about twenty years since the beginning of the modern movement towards the officially sanctioned use of signing in education of deaf children in most programs across the United States. Initially widely heralded as a major advancement (if not a panacea) in educational philosophy and technique, the practice of "Total Communication" (TC) and its results have ultimately turned out to delight some, infuriate others, and thoroughly confuse most of the rest of us. In the beginning, the ideas appeared quite simple to most people:

Accept and use a broader range of communication modes with deaf children, insist no longer on purely oral methods;

Improve children's access to communication and to the structure (and so acquisition) of English by devising ways to represent English manually;

Avoid discouraging or repressing the use of ASL by children (although, within the curriculum, language development efforts would continue to be almost exclusively based on English), and so on.

The movement was supported by a group of studies comparing adolescents: in one line of research adolescents were found to under-stand more information when it was presented with signs than in speech alone; in the second line of research, adolescents who had had different early experiences, including deaf parents and early sign language, outperformed children whose parents were hearing and who had only oral language, etc. (e.g. Stuckless & Birch 1966; Meadow 1968). In the most elaborate of the retrospective comparative studies (Brasel & Quigley 1977), adolescent students were divided into four groups: manual English, ASL, intensive oral, and average oral. The manual English group outperformed all other groups in English syntax, reading, and general achievement. In a study of children from different types of preschools, Moores and his colleagues (Moores, Weiss & Goodwin 1978) found developmental advantages for children in programs using manual communication as compared to children in oral programs.

The implementation of manual English systems led, of course, to a flurry of activity in a two-pronged effort during the 1970s: first, many attempts to formalize or standardize methods for the representation of English, and, second, a mobilization to persuade teachers and parents to use these systems. Relatively few individuals at the time were concerned about such issues as bilingualism (but see Stokoe 1972, Williams 1980), psychological ramifications of bimodality (Ling 1976), the role of ASL in educating deaf children or, for that matter, whether TC as it was first implemented was even physically possible, not to mention effective for instruction. The issue for most people was whether to sign at all, more than the particular way of signing; and most advocates proposed signing simultaneously while speaking. The idea was inherently attractive— for many educators, quite liberating—and so it was not examined quite as critically at first as it was later.

But from the beginning there were doubts about TC, and recently there has been a stir about the practice of TC, lamenting what appears to be a ceiling on the success of education of deaf children. Critical analyses of TC have been presented, and numerous suggestions have been made for changes some more radical than others. A case in point is the recent program paper distributed by members of the Gallaudet University Linguistics Department (Johnson, Liddell & Erting 1989). Among other things, these authors review some of the research on TC and conclude that it is inherently doomed to failure. They indicate that simultaneous communication is "really sign supported speech," (SSS). Indeed, early advocates of simultaneous communication in the education of deaf children, e.g. Gustason (Gustason,

Pfetzing & Zawolkow 1972) and Bornstein (1975), clearly intended for sign to support and clarify speech. Bornstein's early story books included not only illustrations of signs but also pictures of faces with the appropriate mouth shapes. Johnson et al. (1989) offer a counter-proposal that ASL be taught to deaf children as their first language, with English to be taught subsequently as a second language, and this bilingual program be supported by the suppression of simultaneous communication. Attempts at more complete descriptions of signed language in use (e.g., Lucas 1989) are more numerous, although only in their infancy.

In short, there has been considerable critical interest among researchers in analyses of current communication practices—in many cases challenging the basic foundations of the concept of TC as a combination of signing and speaking and as a signed representation of English—and in offering up proposals for change. These researchers focus on several ways of communicating, including codes characterized as Manually Coded English (MCE), Simultaneous Communication (Sim-Com or SC), Signed English, Sign English, signed English, manual English, English signing, Pidgin Sign English (PSE), Ameslish, Siglish, and even "total communication." Whether these are terms naming the same language variety or refer to several different varieties is unclear; the issue of definitions will be a major theme of the discussion to follow. One familiar major controversy, of course, is whether to accept or avoid use of formally-devised manual representations of English. Systems such as Seeing Essential English (SEE$_1$) (Anthony 1971), Signing Exact English (SEE$_2$) (Gustason, Pfetzing & Zawolkow 1972), and Linguistics of Visual English (Wampler 1971) have come in for heavy criticism on a number of grounds (e.g. Baker & Cokely 1980, Wilbur 1979, Ramsey 1989). But this line of research is much broader and deeper than that. It goes to a basic set of questions about: (1) the general concept of signing and speaking at the same time, (2) signed representation of the segmental structure of English, (3) pidginization processes in language contact and multilingualism, (4) principles of instruction and methods of teaching language to young deaf children, and (5) the ethics and politics of particular language policies.

There are numerous varieties of simultaneous communication and of codes for English. It is not clear to what extent these two overlap. Certainly, one is an issue of mode to use and the is a segmental language issue, but they are usually discussed as if they are inseparable. Are all forms of simultaneous communi-cation and systems for representing English subject to the same criticisms? What, exactly, happens in simultaneous communication in its various forms? Can we (should we?) establish what is correct? "Correct" in what sense? How communicative is simultaneous communication? What do people actually do, in practice, when they speak words and sign signs simultaneously? How useful are various forms of simultaneous communication and English-representing systems for social communication, for instruction, for language acquisition? What is the relation between simultaneous communication and spoken or written English? Between simultaneous communication and ASL? Is simultaneous communication always or truly a pidgin, Pidgin Sign English (PSE)? If so, what processes are occurring? What relationships obtain among the varieties of language in the Deaf Community?

On another level, how ethical or moral is it to take the language of a minority group (the Deaf) and manipulate that language to represent the language of the majority group (the hearing)? Who should make such decisions? Should a manual code for English be a part of communication practices in programs for deaf students? How does the use of simultaneous communication (in any form) fit into various proposals for bilingual (ASL/English) education of deaf students?

In any attempt to address these questions we are confronted with three basic issues: I, the description of natural language practices in the community, II, the effectiveness of language practices for English language development, and III, the ethics of particular language policies. The research examining these issues and various proposals for change varies widely in scope, depth, and acceptance.

In this paper much of this work is reviewed in an effort to clarify issues and frame some of the basic questions in a way that may be helpful for a fuller understanding of the contributions of research and its relevance for school programs. The plan is to present first the proposed solutions and the grounds for criticism that have motivated the desire for change. The discussion then focuses on two linguistic questions that have been confused in the literature to date: first, the question of language representation in more than one modality is addressed; second, a discussion of the possible outcomes of language contact follows—including some attention to pidgin and creole languages and multilingualism. The final section of the paper presents a consideration of the implications of the proposals for change in light of the linguistic principles and social contexts.

Four types of proposals for change

The roots of some of this work go back to the 1960s—not to mention the early 1900s in the U.S. or de l'Epee's time at the end of the 1700s in France (Lane 1985). Of course, there have been significant changes in the basic underlying premises and issues examined since that time. At present, a recurring theme in the research literature is one of dissatisfaction with current communication practices in the education of deaf children. Exactly what one is dissatisfied *about*, however, varies. In addition to calls to eliminate signing completely, proposals for how to deal with the situation fall into four basic types, each of which will be examined more closely below.

The first, lamenting the skills of most teachers and parents of deaf children, calls for better training and commitment and for national standardization. The second set of proposals questions whether segmental matching of spoken and signed structure simultaneously is possible or practicable and suggests various modifications in simultaneous communication. Some of these proposals call for greater "incorporation of ASL features" in simultaneous communication or for eliminating the voice (e.g. Strong & Charlson 1989). The third calls for a greater separation between English and ASL in some kind of bilingual format. Sometimes simultaneous communication is included as the form of English, and sometimes English is restricted to speech and writing (Stokoe 1972, Bouvet 1982, Luetke-Stahlman 1983, Strong 1988). The fourth set of proposals is to change the relation between English and ASL in education, to establish ASL as the first language and the primary teaching language and to provide instruction in English as a second language in the curriculum (Johnson et al. 1989).

Evaluation of the proposals

How might we evaluate the merits of proposals such as these? How can we think through the various proposals and related research reports? Indeed, how can we even conduct fruitful discussions about them? Communication mode and language use pose a critical problem for the field, yet there are few topics which generate more confusion and extremes of emotion than this one.

The major sources of difficulty group themselves into the three kinds of issues introduced above: linguistic description, instructional effectiveness, and politics. They are further confounded by considerable slipperiness in definitions. It is often quite difficult (if not impossible at times) to know just what form of com-munication authors are referring to in their writing, and there is tremendous variety in the actual practice of signing as well as in the terms used to refer to it. Natural variation, which occurs both within a community of language users or code users and within an individual, is a factor to be considered carefully in these matters; it is often overlooked. Despite the collective efforts of researchers over the past two decades, we still lack adequate descriptive data on use, comprehension, and eventual educational conse-quences of using signs and speech together and of signed representations of English. Although there are notable exceptions, such as some of the work of Erting (1983, 1985a,b), Lee (1983), and

Lucas and Valli (1989), research and theory are insufficiently data driven. The proposals suggesting what are loosely termed bilingual approaches to educating deaf students need clarification as to the concepts and terms used in the discussions. Furthermore, many scholars and edu-cators are drawing conclusions about instructional effectiveness without describing instructional effects. There are many more claims of incompre-hensibility than studies of comprehension of specific elements. Finally, the topic of communication mode has some serious ethical and sociopolitical dimensions involving the community and culture of deaf individuals. Sensitivity to these concerns must accompany inves-tigation of language in the schools and community; yet how much of a driving force will be behind policy recommendations and how policy will interact with the process of scientific inquiry and scholarship are political questions. Outcomes are not just a matter of functional skill development but of identify and basic social values (Ramsey 1989, Maxwell & Kraemer in press). These issues are not fully independent of each other, and together may account for much of the difficulty experienced in confronting the issue of the communication mode to use in education of deaf children. It seems impossible to investigate language in deaf adults or children without facing the fact that one's research results will be perceived as political moves in the education debate.

In the final section of this paper, each of the current proposals for change will be more thoroughly examined. Since the proposals to "do something" about the use of manual forms of English communication presuppose that there is something wrong to be corrected, it is worth starting with the descriptions of communication that have been generated thus far.

What is "wrong" with simcom?

As alluded to already, one researcher's characterization of manually coded English (MCE), for example, can be quite different from another's: e.g. one uses ASL signs to represent English words (just as they are conventionally spelled in print), another uses invented signs to represent all English morphemes. The term Pidgin Sign English (PSE) has been used extensively in writing on this subject, but with little data to support definitions or distinguish PSE from non-fluent MCE. Sometimes writers attempt to define what they are referring to; at other times a term is used with no specification whatsoever. The designation MCE seems to focus on the components of English represented in the sign channel alone. Simultaneous communication focuses on bimodality. PSE focuses on finding in signing elements of ASL, of English, and of certain linguistic processes characteristic of pidgin languages.

What is seen as a "deficiency" in the practice of bimodality depends in large part on what a particular author deems to be the purpose of the use of this form of communication. For example, a number of early studies (e.g. Crandall 1978, Marmor & Pettito 1979, Kluwin 1981, Swisher 1983) presupposed that the "correct" form of bimodality is an exact manual representation of all English morphemes presented simultaneously in sign and in speech. Most often the variety of signing in mind was something like Signing Exact English (SEE$_2$) (Gustason et al. 1972), where there is supposed to be a signed morpheme corresponding to each spoken morpheme, including the full range of English affixes and inflectional forms. Several other invented forms of manually coded English—e.g. Seeing Essential English (SEE$_1$) (Anthony 1971), Linguistics of Visual English (Wampler 1971), and Signed English (Bornstein 1975)—would fall in this category, too. The idea was that this visual representation of the spoken morphology of English would be more effectively available to deaf children than speech alone, thus aiding in their acquisition of English.

The emphasis in these systems and, consequently in the research, is on English spoken (and signed) *morphology*. It was soon clear to most observers that few individuals were consistently faithful to these systems; most people appear to find it difficult at best to coordinate their speech and "exact" signing, and tend not to sign every morphological detail of the English sentence being uttered. Inconsistencies have been described in the communication of hearing parents (Crandall 1978, Swisher & Thompson 1985) and teachers (Marmor & Petitto 1979, Kluwin 1981, Bernstein, Maxwell & Matthews 1985), of deaf adults (Lee 1983, Maxwell & Bernstein 1985), of deaf children of hearing parents (Schlesinger & Meadow 1972 Raffin, Davis & Gilman 1978, Crandall 1978, Bornstein & Saulnier 1981, Bornstein, Saulnier & Hamilton 1980, S. Supalla 1986), and of deaf children of deaf parents (Maxwell 1987). Notably Supalla (1986) claims that children not only delete the English bound morphemes from their talk but that they are "devising spatially-based grammatical devices even when they have not been exposed to any." In addition, there are anomalies in the use of the invented signs by some children (Maxwell 1987) and in speech some characteristic distortions of intonation, phrasing, and pronunciation that have yet to receive systematic study (Maxwell & Cannito, in progress), although the widespread assumption is that the effect of the signing on speech is negative.

On the morphological level of its own goals, then, of course, this approach is a failure, since the morphological details of English are not consistently all available to the receiver, and furthermore, attempts to make them so seem to interfere with communication in other ways. Even if many individuals sign with speech as intended, the approach is intended for everyone; so must be judged on its general success. By this standard, the impression is that the success level is low. In this context, then, researchers set out to assess the degree to which the sign and speech morphology correspond in samples of individuals practicing bimodal communication. The basic strategy was to conduct a morphological analysis of the English speech of a few hearing adults in a sample of utterances, looking for the presence and "accuracy" of the corresponding sign representations of the English morphemes. Mismatches between the spoken and signed morphemes, and omissions from sign of morphemes that are spoken were tallied and "accuracy" scores derived.

These studies not surprisingly revealed quite a degree of "inaccuracy," mostly omissions in the sign channel of morphemes that were spoken. Quite simply in these samples users of simultaneous speech and sign did not always sign the same elements of the English sentences as they said them—at least as compared to a 1:1 correspondence of sign morphemes (invented or borrowed from ASL) to speech morphemes of English. Based on just the signs of the sentences, the grammar often appeared quite truncated, almost telegraphic—and certainly did not always fully represent the surface structure of the spoken sentences. Systematic descriptions of the phenomenon were for the most part restricted to categorizing and tallying deletions and mismatches by English morphological and syntactic classes. The conclusions drawn were that bimodal language was erratic and inconsistent.

Another disturbing and puzzling characteristic of hearing teachers' bimodal communication emerged in a comparison of teachers' communication in oral and total communication (TC) classrooms (Newton 1985). TC teachers reported that they avoided producing utterances they did not know how to sign. They revealed confusion about the basis for signing correctly. They were unsure of what a sign represented: an ASL word, a "concept," an English word—and indeed, samples of the English of the TC teachers were less idiomatic than those of the oral teachers interviewed for the study. Newton assumes these adaptations mean that oral teachers are presenting an English interaction style more facilitative for language acquisition than TC teachers. Her study, however, fails to gauge comprehension or to rate the children's part of the interaction. Findings such as these have led to sweeping conclusions about the use of bimodal communication in classroom situations and by parents and have resulted in two types of recommendations.

Some (Marmor & Petitto 1979, Kluwin 1981, Strong & Charlson 1989) have claimed that simultaneous communication as practiced by teachers presents an ungrammatical and virtually unintelligible input to students, neither corresponding to the grammar of ASL nor to that of English and therefore worse than useless. As such, they argue, it would be virtually worthless as an aid to language acquisition in deaf children and should either be eliminated altogether or dropped in favor of ASL, a natural language. Simultaneous communication and manually coded English systems are often referred to as "auxiliary languages in the sense that they are contrived (artificial) codes purposely invented to serve specific communicative and educational functions" (Bochner & Albertini 1988: 8). There is a sense that ASL has inherent advantages simply because it is a natural language as compared to a coded one (Strong & Charlson 1989, Strong 1988, and Johnson et al. 1989).

The other position corresponds to a "training" proposal (Swisher, 1983, Swisher & Thompson, 1985, Gaustad 1986). Using essentially the same sort of approach to the description of bimodal speech and sign, proponents of this view also consider bimodal use to be "deficient" but call for its better use. Swisher has analyzed data collected from hearing mothers of deaf children and explained its structure on the basis of the difficulties the hearing mothers have in learning to communicate bimodally, and suggests that we need to do a better job training them. Gaustad (1986) echoes this view and adds that the child's acquisition is directly related to the quantity and quality of input. The basic premises are: (a) that the purpose of bimodality is to represent content words, function words, and bound morphemes of English exactly, and (b) that the lack of exact correspondence, at the morphological level, between the sign and speech is "bad." These premises are unchallenged.

Semantic analysis & bimodality

In reviewing the early studies, it became clear to Mark Bernstein and me that something was seriously out of kilter. We had certainly seen some rotten communication in classrooms, too; but anyone who has observed very many deaf individuals communicating with each other and with hearing individuals has seen tremendous variation in communication codes. As has been pointed out time and again, often (though not always) both the hearing and deaf individuals converse in what appears to be at least an attempt at English while signing—the hearing person may speak and the deaf person may speak or silently mouth the words—but not necessarily representing all the same grammatical details in both modes. Deaf individuals sometimes communicate with each other in a similar fashion (Brasel & Quigley 1977, Lucas & Valli 1989, Winston 1989). And this form of bimodality seemed to bear some resemblance to what was being described in the early literature on English signed in classrooms. The point is that there are at least some varieties of bimodal speech-sign communication that are used by hearing and deaf individuals quite effectively, and it is hard to see how this could be possible if the relationship between the sign and speech was always as poor as suggested by the studies cited above. Furthermore, it seems rather dangerous to make assumptions about what *receivers* of communication (in whatever form, children or adults) make of it in comprehension, especially since there is so much evidence that children derive more information when sign is added to speech. If we are not to jump at the whim of educational fashion designers, we need much more information about the details of production, comprehension, and interaction.

This observation, among other thoughts, led us to extend the analysis of simultaneous speech and sign. Oddly enough, the characteristics of deaf individuals' simultaneous communication had been ignored. We were interested in simultaneous speech and sign as used by deaf as well as hearing individuals, both in and outside of classrooms (Maxwell & Bernstein, 1985, Bernstein, Maxwell & Matthews, 1985; Maxwell, Bernstein & Matthews in press). We looked for correspondence at the morphological level, as had previous researchers, but we added the dimension of semantics—at the utterance and discourse levels.

Rather than prejudge that *any* deviation from exact sign–speech morpheme correspondence is "bad," we attempted to assess the degree to which the sign and speech channels correspond at the level of the *message*, and we chose as consultants individuals (deaf and hearing) who were fluent and comfortable in everyday bimodal English communication. Our data revealed the usual pattern of morphological mismatch, mostly deletions. No surprises there, although the situation appeared less idiosyncratic than previously reported. There were some patterns in common across signers. At the message level, though, we found a remarkable fit between the sign and speech. In essence, it is not at all an *inevitable* conclusion that the use of bimodal language presents incoherent, unintelligible or confusing input to receivers. Data supporting this view have emerged in recent work by Gallagher and Meador (1989) and have been discussed in a paper by Eagney (1987).

How might it be possible that bimodality functions communicatively even in the absence of "exact" correspondence? To fully understand this, we suggested (1) that we must be careful about the consultants selected for study (ours were fluent deaf adults as well as hearing teachers, engaged in informal peer conversation as well as instruction), and (2) that looking at the "grammaticality" of the sign channel alone (as in previous studies) misses a lot of what is going on. One must look at the synergy between the two channels in this bimodal form of communication. In agreement with some of the early studies, we suggested that there are psycholinguistic processing constraints on bimodal production; something has to give when one attempts to use both speech and sign simultaneously with such a large number of segmented units. This point has had strong support over the years (see Bellugi & Fischer 1972, Kluwin 1981, Wilbur 1987). It appeared that in the particular form of bimodality we investigated (informal con-versations and classroom use by hearing teachers and deaf adolescents and teachers), production was essentially English based; the underlying English sentence was fully expressed orally (or silently mouthed, in the case of one deaf teacher), while a somewhat more skeletal form, preserving the key phrase structure elements, was expressed in the signing. The basic pattern of deletions we observed involved just those elements that are the "fine–tuning" aspects of English surface structure—the many functors, affixes, agreement markers, and the like, which are always vulnerable to loss under pressure (Slobin & Welsh 1973). Yet these elements in our data were (a) almost always present and available in the speech (for reception via speech reading or audition); *and* (b) recoverable in some sense from the context of the conversation. Of course, one must know the language well to make use of the information in these elements, but many deaf individuals do. They are fluent in English but are unable to hear it (Davis 1989).

The point is that even omissions in the sign channel of signed tokens for morphemes that are spoken do not necessarily lead to drastic semantic difficulty or conflict. It depends on the particular deletion *taken in context* in the conversational setting. In addition these bimodal communicators typically produce the English vocally (or at least on the lips), and many deaf individuals do indeed make some use of this information in reception. The comprehension of different individuals of signs and speech in bimodal communication should be investigated.

There is confusion in some professional discussions between comprehension and acquisition. That is, when one knows a language, one understands abbreviations, ellipses, etc. (which is why an adult losing her hearing comprehends speech better than a deaf child), and, indeed, one may understand some elliptical language better than some redundant language. The impact on acquisition of rampant abbreviations and ellipses may be another story.[1]

---

[1] Chomsky (1965) thought it astounding that children could learn to speak with an input full of false starts, ellipsis, etc. Much time has been expended by researchers convinced of the importance of environment to show that hearing children's input is *not* so lacking. Maybe we've found the limit of the

Far from being the last word on descriptions of bimodality, the work reviewed in this section suggests just the contrary; that we've only just begun to gather information to help us understand how bimodal language (in any form) functions as a communication mode, much less know how it performs as the source of language acquisition. What this line of descriptive work does do, though, is raise a number of questions and cautions in connection with the ways bimodality and English signing have been discussed recently. Among these are such concerns as the extent of variation across individuals, groups, and contexts; the nomenclature problem (What is being referred to when writers criticize, or support,the use of MCE, SC, SEE, etc.?); and the still-missing analyses of compre-hension processes. On this last point, the closest the field has come thus far to comprehension studies is quite preliminary. Hatfield, Caccamise & Siple (1978) reported that for adolescents who were fluent in ASL to some degree, there seemed to be no differences in comprehension of stories presented either in ASL or in "MCE." Eagney (1987) and Kidd (1988), for example, tested comprehension of sentences presented in three different forms (ASL, some form of "simplified"

---

conditions on acquisition that the environmentalists started looking for—most deaf children's English input is too bad to support language acquisition!!!

MCE, and "standard" segmental representation of English). They also found no differences. The best we might be able to conclude at this point is that there does not as yet appear to be any evidence to suggest that bimodality (however characterized) cannot function for effective communication.

Of course, none of these criticisms would elicit such widespread response if deaf children's achievement levels had risen noticeably. Instead, we find that the average achievement scores on the SAT hover about where they were before the Total Communication revolution. People may be fractious because there is growing consensus that neither promise of the 1970s—TC, nor mainstreaming—has borne the fruit of better educational results. Children's inconsistent use of the invented English morpheme signs in appropriate linguistic contexts (Raffin, Davis & Gilman 1978, Bornstein & Saulnier 1981, Bornstein, Saulnier & Hamilton 1980) has also discouraged advocates. Maxwell characterized the use of bound morpheme signs by some young deaf children(1987), and the written use of bound morphemes and functors by some deaf adolescents who could not take dictation from their own teacher (1983b), more as discourse markers of English style than as grammatical morphemes. That is, these children used inflectional and derivational morphemes and functors liberally but oddly, sometimes independently of root words, and seemed to use them more to mean 'this is English' than to carry specific semantic or grammatical information. On the other hand, hearing mothers and their preschool deaf children using bimodal communication show more fluency and positive affect in dyadic communication than mothers and oral children (e.g. Greenberg 1980, 1983). Affect, fluency, and rich semantic content were addressed by Schlesinger and Meadow (1972), along with linguistic structure. Their four children were progressing well in all domains. Audiences of parents and professionals viewing Schesinger's and Gustason's videotapes in programs around the country were audibly amazed at the English fluency of the children and, even more, perhaps, at the range and depth of topics, including life in foreign countries and interpersonal relationships. Analysis of classroom interaction, conversational abilities, and topic analysis might well be in order to derive a better understanding of the uses of bimodal communication and English representation.

Language representation

Implicit in the previous discussion is an underlying difference in the goals of bimodality, as viewed by different researchers and policy makers. Those who focus on the quality of language input to deaf children have emphasized the sign channel alone and the aspects of morphology evident in English speech but not reliably evident in the signs. Those concerned with understanding the nature of fluent language and bimodality *per se* emphasize the communicativeness. The two goals may lead to some confusion. For example, critiques of bimodal input inexplicably but typically (e.g. Strong 1988, Johnson et al. 1989) omit consideration of the work on fluent bimodality. Wise consideration and evaluation of the potential of bimodality as input, however, must consider actual practice of fluent adults as well as the language of children in these linguistic environments. While it is true that artificial codes were deliberately invented for instruction and are not the natural results of linguistic change, they use many elements of natural language, and some invented signs have become quite widely used. The point is not necessarily to copy what adults do—after all, mothers do not talk to their infants the way they talk to their adult friends— but to avoid saying about what is and is not possible foolish things that may devalue adult language. Deaf people have suffered enough devaluation of their communication, after all.

The concept of fit between modes of representation: A detour through the history of writing

One of the issues in understanding bimodality concerns the fit between speech and sign. *Fit* is a concept that is usually employed in discussions of writing systems (Gelb 1952); applying it to sign systems provides some important insight. There's a famous and delightful anonymous paper[1] making fun of using signs to represent English by comparing it to using French morphemes to represent English; this idea has influenced thinking about representation, pidgins, and total communication. Consequently, it is worth while to consider in some depth how a language medium or mode (speech, writing, signing)represents language (Baron 1981, Crystal 1987).

Although alphabetic writing is the most common system of graphemic representation in the modern era, there are a number of other options. Writing systems can fit different aspects of talk, including reference meaning or word meaning, or they can fit different aspects of the sound of language.

> Writing can never be considered an *exact* counterpart of the spoken language. Such an ideal state of point-by-point equivalence in which one speech unit is expressed by one sign, and one sign expresses only one speech unit, has never been attained in writing. (Gelb 1952: 15)

A quick review of some different ways in which speech and print can fit yields levels that can be applied to sign and speech as well.

The main distinction is between phonological and non-phonological systems. Pictographs are, or course,

---

[1] The editor has good evidence for attributing the authorship of this paper to Harry Markowicz of the Gallaudet University English Department. See also SLS 68: 195-217.

quite pictorial, but they are considered non-phono-logical writing. The fit between pictographs and referential meanings is close, but the fit between pictographs and spoken sentences is extremely loose. That is, readers can interpret what pictographs mean and all interpret the same meaning, but readers telling that meaning are not likely to speak the same sentences, possibly not even the same language. Eight different spoken languages in China are very different from each other in vocabulary and pronunciation; nevertheless, they have all been considered Chinese because of the single method of writing all of them and a common literary and cultural history. Logographies such as Chinese have a close fit with words and parts of words but a very loose fit with sounds. That is, the reader can identify the word represented by a logograph, but speakers of different Chinese dialects, for example, may speak different words. Some words may be unrelated in their spoken forms, even though each one matches the written word. Chinese logographs do include some phonological information, but that will "count" for speakers of some dialects reading them and not for some others.

Syllabaries and alphabets have close fits with the sounds of the spoken language, but with different units or levels of sound. Syllabaries are comprised of graphic symbols that fit syllables rather than individual phonemes. Syllabaries are one of the most persistent kinds of systems, ranging from sixth century B.C. Cyprus to modern Japanese kata-kana. The number of graphemes in a syllabary is anything from fifty to several hundred (Crystal 1987: 201). Alphabets are abstracted lists of graphemic symbols for phonemes ranging from eleven letters in a Solomon Islands language to seventy-four in Khmer. Most contain twenty to thirty graphemes; alphabets are also historically influenced, so that modern alphabets are not much like transcription systems. They are favored in the modern era for several reasons:

1. It is relatively easy to create an alphabet for a language whose speakers have not already developed a writing system for themselves (Bible translators in this century have created alphabets for dozens of languages that never had writing systems);
2. It is easy to learn to make the letters (though not always to spell conventionally) and does not demand artistic ability or special materials;
3. It is easy to transfer the alphabet code to other communication means such as semaphores and telegraphs;
4. Nations with alphabets have dominated the world order and world trade. More recently, it is easy to transfer the alphabet to other technologies such as typewriters and computers.

Schmandt-Besserat (1982) has revolutionized our understanding of early writing systems by showing that the earliest ones may have had nothing at all to do with speech but were codes for certain ideas that merchants and traders had difficulty remembering, such as the prices in a deal for sheep or pots. It is only with alphabets that we gain the concept of writing *as speech written down* and thus the concept of a close fit between speech and writing.

Studies of comparative reading and writing indicate that with alphabets the advantage is with the writer, while in logographic systems there is some advantage to the reader. That is, alphabets make it easy and fast to write, but hard and slow to read; logographies are faster and easier to read but slow to write. Japanese, for example, which has available logographs, a syllabary, and an alphabet, uses different writing systems at different points in the process of reading instruction and uses a combination of logographs and the syllabary for the newspaper. Japan apparently has virtually no problem with literacy. At the other extreme, China has only a logography. Reading is aided by this system, but writing (not to mention computerization) is greatly slowed. Another difference is in learning; alphabets are less of a learning challenge than logographies, so the system for reading and writing can be more efficiently taught.

Spelling conventions use alphabets to represent words but not individual sounds. Conventions determine how close will be the fit between the orthography and speech. Alphabets are not phonetic or phonemic transcription systems; e.g. some alphabets "don't bother" with vowels. Arabic, Hebrew, and Aramaic have systems of optional diacritical markings that clue the reader to the vowels. All alphabets are not the same, and languages that use the same alphabet, e.g. Spanish and English, do not use exactly the same letters or use the letters to represent exactly the same sounds. Spanish and English both write <rr>, but speakers of the two languages pronounce the sound represented differently. The Russian alphabet has more letters than the alphabet in this text; consequently some sounds that we would represent with blends or with two letters, such as /ts/ and /ch/ are represented by single letters. As Gelb observes, even the:

> wide acceptance of the Latin alphabet in modern times has led to no unity. In many cases the signs of the Latin alphabet received widely variant phonetic values in different countries... The limitless homophony of signs is best illus-trated by the spellings of...Chekhov, in which the initial sound can be written as ch, tch, c, tsch, tsi, ti, tj, sc, or c.... (1952:240)

English is notorious for the weak fit between the alphabet and speech caused by our spelling conventions. Even within English there are 13.7 spellings per sound and 3.5 sounds per letter (Dewey 1971). George Bernard Shaw is credited with an outrageous spelling of *fish* as *ghoti* —*f* as in *cough*, *i* as in *women*, and *sh* as in *nation*. English is not really as unpredictable as that: 84% of words are spelled according to a regular pattern and only 3% are completely unpredictable. Furthermore, most irregularly spelled words are also the most common words (Hanna, Hodges, & Hanna 1971). Various attempts to change spelling to make the fit closer arise regularly. Some reformed spellings, like *catalog* and *dialog* and *nite* are successful, at least in advertising and informal writing, but others are resisted, especially those related to word derivations. Nation/nationality/nationalize are not likely to emerge any time soon, if ever, as *naishun/nashonality/nashunalize*. The spelling system in fact conveys information that speech does not and thus allows readers and writers to perceive connections between words and to see the history of their language (Chomsky & Halle 1968). Besides, if we did not have conventionalized spelling, people would have to "sound out" everything they read, which would slow reading down dramatically. Conservatism, conveni-ence, and historical awareness together conspire to resist most spelling reform.

Languages "borrow" each others' writing systems all the time. Alphabets are commonly appropriated from one language to serve another and vary greatly in the regularity of correspondence between graphemes and phonemes. Around 1700 B. C. the

North Semitic alphabet, using twenty-two consonant letters, appeared. The symbols were taken by speakers of Hebrew, Arabic, and Phoenician for their use. The Greeks added vowels to the Phoenician list about 1000 B.C. About two hundred years after that the Etruscans borrowed Greek writing; Etruscan led to early and modern Latin, which is the basis of all modern Western alphabets. The Roman alphabet is common all over the world now, partly because it is the one the (European and American) Bible translators took with them all over the world and because it is efficient. The Japanese took their logography from the Chinese in about the eighth century. That is, they took the symbols and their meanings, but when the Japanese read the logographs, they spoke Japanese. Over time, the two writing systems have diverged, but the origin is still evident.

Once a language has adopted a writing system, the language changes, because of the mutual influences in the interrelation between speech and writing. Languages with phonetic writing, like English, resist phonetic and morphological change, while languages with non-phonetic writing are more likely to change rapidly and to break up into diverse and even mutually unintelligible dialects. To adopt a theory of language representation is not to ignore the constraints of modality on language. Indeed, transferring language to new modalities and to new writing systems within a modality necessarily brings about change in a language. Written phonetic abbreviations, (*ammo* for ammunition), acronyms (*snafu* for 'situation normal, all fouled up,' *radar* for 'radio detection and ranging,' and "alphabetisms" (*VIP* pronounced "vee eye pee") are sources of new spoken words. Written syntax may develop quite differently from spoken syntax. And certain poetic forms arise only with writing (Bright 1982). Pictorial writing may convey more information more efficiently than speech. In Egyptian pictorial writing, e.g. *a vase*, ambiguous in the spoken form would not only be expressed in terms of color, size, and shape, but also perhaps through the use of a determinative for stone or metal added to the picture (Gelb 1952: 229).

Thus, the history of writing systems makes it clear that it is not uncommon to take a representational system from one language and use it to represent another one. (The donor group will either show pride, resentment, or indifference because of social conditions—not because of linguistic ones. And, of course, at first few people will know the new system, presenting a learning need or an opportunity for rejection, and the system will change to adapt to the new language.) If we think of MCE as a representational system, then there is no *linguistic* reason why signs cannot be taken and modified to represent

English. But then the question is, to represent which parts of English?

Although writing *can be* speech written down, it is well recognized that writing is not fully and accurately described as speech written down. Speech and writing both are English, but different information, different styles of information conveyance, different linguistic structures, etc. are represented in the two modes on an oral-to-literate continuum (e.g. Tannen 1982). One often cited difference is the role of intonation. Intonation is a major conveyor of information,both syntactic and attitudinal, in speech but not in writing. Yet no one says that writing is ungrammatical and uncommunicative because it does not convey all of the information that speech conveys. Analysis focuses on what aspects of English are represented in the two different modes of speech and writing.

The fit of speech & sign

To what extent is the fit between speech and writing an analogue that applies to sign and speech? It has often been said that MCE inventors took the lexicon of one language (ASL) and applied the morphology of another (English), which seems like a pretty out-rageous thing to do. But is it more outrageous than taking the writing system of one language and using it to represent another? Are we confusing a political outrage having to do with language dominance and cultural hegemony with a linguistic inanity? Perhaps this is why most hearing people and English-oriented deaf people appear comfortable with MCE. They are appropriating fingerspelling and signs from ASL to represent English as people have for centuries appropriated others' writing systems to represent their own languages. There's no inherent reason why signs cannot represent English, just as writing represents English. Thus there are three questions about the representation of English in sign. (1) Is this the politically and ethically correct thing to do? (2) What aspects of English structure will be closely represented and which aspects will be distorted or lost? and (3) Since languages and systems change to adapt to new modalities, what aspects of structure, style, and use will change between spoken and signed English?

From this perspective, let us reconsider the invented MCE experiment. The political-ethical issue is a hard one for hearing researchers to say anything sensible about. After all, we are the larger group, we don't have any problem having our language represented in a third mode (sign), but we must be sensitive to minority groups' attitudes toward their own language. Many deaf individuals are hurt and angered by this use of ASL while others see the events as interesting and even positive changes (e.g. Ramsey 1989). One can hardly find a forum attended

by deaf persons in which heated comments on the subject do not come up. Furthermore, there is an undercurrent of fear that ASL will disappear. Investigation of the political and ethical issues involved in this manipulation by those who are better equipped to offer it should continue.

From the point of view of English structure, we can ask, what are the possible levels of fit between speech and sign? Levels of structure include discourse, message, sentence constituent, word, morphology and word structure, word sounds and word spelling, intonation and phrasing. For some reason, from the beginning of the experiment, the inventors got stuck on the level of morphology and word structure. Some of the system devisers are concerned also with word sounds and word spelling; hence the "two out of three rule" for selecting a sign for a spoken word[1], Naturally, since that was the level at which MCE, SEE$_1$, and SEE$_2$, etc. presented themselves in the 70s, that was the level at which using them was evaluated. None of the systems is a perfect morphological match. People do not consistently use the invented morphemes available to them, and the signs for the morphemes function in a structurally anomalous way. The invented MCE systems all rely on *linear*

---

[1] E.g. if the English words sound the same and are spelled the same, like directional *right* and correct *right*, then one sign is used for both meanings.

affixation, adding prefixes and suffixes to words. Many writers have observed that producing these forms from a system overtly learned rather than acquired over time forces a considerable and unnatural degree of metalinguistic awareness and intentional analysis on interaction. Presumably children exposed to such signing as input would, however, naturally acquire the system, as hearing English acquirers produce correct forms and apply "rules" before they are able consciously to analyze their own language productions. It is a truism that speakers produce far more complex grammar than linguists can derive rules for. But apparently neither children nor adults consistently apply linear affixation. S. Supalla (1990) argues that the constraints of the sign modality preclude linear affixation, and our information on the world's sign languages is that, as far as is now known, none employs linear affixation. If that analysis of mode constraints proves true, then the inclusion of linear affixes in a sign representation system will not be successful (i.e. lasting). Print systems do not include much prosodic information, even though reading print requires that a reader supply it. Perhaps the constraints of print are that prosody is not worth the effort of representation in such a system. Similarly, perhaps linear affixations are not worth the unnatural effort of representation in a sign system.

On the other hand, bimodality (speech with signs) preceded any of these invented sign representation systems; so the primary concept of combining modes is not a result of the movement to invent sign codes. One earnestly wishes that there had been research on bimodal communication and English sign representation before the inventors of these systems tried to "improve" on this natural behavior by introducing new signing systems. What, really, did those deaf parents do to communicate manually in English? Today the invented signs are widely known, even if not widely used. English linear affixes are poorly represented; nevertheless, how do MCE and bimodality of various kinds do at levels other than morphological? Which levels are most important to successful interaction? to input for language acquisition?

At the intonation and phrasing level, although there are no studies to evaluate, certainly we have all heard some bimodal communication that has a flat inton-ation and has word–by–word phrasing rather than phrasing according to sentence constituents and semantics. What of it? According to Peters (1983), for example, intonation and phrasing are crucial for young children's acquisition, for it is from phrasing and intonation that children first separate out words and other units of language. The different rates of sign and speech production (Baker 1978, Bellugi & Fischer 1972, Grosjean 1977) may explain the odd cadence of bimodality, since stringing sequential hand signs together actually takes longer than stringing sequential voice morphemes together—perhaps too long to be held in short term memory or too awkward to be phrased appropriately. On the other hand, clear speech that is intelligible to hard of hearing individuals is slower and has other differences from conversational speech (Picheny, Durlach & Braida 1985, 1986, 1989). How much are elements of MCE or bimodality the result of stress on the modes, of lack of fluency, or of deliberate adaptations to be clear? At the sentence constituent level, how does bimodality work? Apparently, from the available research, speech and sign constituents have a close fit for fluent users but a poor fit for the non-fluent. At the sign and word level, the fit is strong. Between word sounds and word spelling there is virtually no fit. And so on. A complete analysis remains to be done. The point is that MCE can represent English at different levels besides that of morpheme-to-morpheme correspondence.

If training is to be undertaken for teachers and parents, should the emphasis be on bound morphemes, on clear messages, on intonation and phrasing, on spelling? We have done a lot of talking about normal language acquisition in this field; perhaps we need to revisit that literature to think about aspects of language and characteristics of input that appear to be most closely related to language acquisition. They appear to be those aspects that communicate semantic information, attract attention, and engage a conversational partner's interest, at least at the early stages, more than those aspects that focus on morphological inflections (See e.g. Snow 1977, Cross 1978). And then we must consider how to deal with those aspects of English that are lost or distorted. Can they be sacrificed? Can they be taught through print, or through later instruction?

If indeed bimodality, at least in some uses, consists of spoken plus signed representations of English, then it makes sense to compare those representations, to conventionalize the fit between sign and speech and sign and writing, and to teach children what that fit is, as we have to teach them the relation between speech and writing. We do not criticize print on the basis that it has to be learned, indeed learning to read it is a major goal of schooling; yet we assume that deaf children will figure out for themselves the relation among these three modes. Why should representation work without instruction in all three modes? A child might understand the sign DENY without knowing how to write it or vice versa, just as a hearing person might be able to say *Aloysius* without knowing how to write it or read *epitome* without knowing how to say it. The differences as well as the similarities in language in all three modes could be taught to children. How would deaf children learn, for instance, the role of intonation in syntactic phrasing and the levels of colloquial politeness in spoken language? the levels of formality, conventional spelling, anaphora (e.g. pronouns), and morphology in writing? And how would they learn connections between these elements of language and signed communication?

For at least some communicators, combining two modes of representation, instead of leading to exact duplication, leads to a synergistic sharing of the load of representing underlying English-encoded messages. Bimodality is long–lived and probably here to stay in some shape, even if it is excluded from classroom instruction. We need to identify communicative prac-tices that enhance and those that impede comprehen-sion for different individuals, and we need to understand how bimodality works. For example, Alice, a deaf child in a deaf home, used bimodality as well as speech alone and sign alone for interaction. Switching modes gave her not only communicative options, but the switch itself became a key for certain messages (Maxwell 1983a, 1989). What are the characteristics of the linguistic repertoires of other deaf children? Alice sorted her way through bimodality and bilingualism, but other deaf children seem to have virtually no idea of the sign representation system for English that their hearing teachers assume to be part of their competence (Maxwell 1983b). Moreover, many interpreter clients complain on a similar basis (Kuykendall 1990).

Outcomes of language contact

The transfer and adaptation of a writing system from one group to another is one possible outcome of language contact. Thus the Japanese appropriated Chinese logography without the cooperation of the Chinese, and the Roman alphabet has been used to write numerous non–Romance languages. *In the case of signs, though, the language of ASL may go along with the medium of signs.* That is, when a sign is used to represent an English word, it still represents an ASL word, too, because there are ASL speakers in the community. Although some deaf children have no exposure to ASL, signs are being used as the medium for two languages in this community, both for ASL and for English. Most of the objection to using signs to represent English includes claims that there is incoherent language mixing, often inadvertent on the part of hearing signers. Therefore, we must consider not only the issue of language representation but also language mixing and bilingualism.

Bilingualism or even multilingualism in a country is actually more common than monolingualism. There are fewer than two hundred countries and about five thousand languages. Thus there is a great deal of language contact in the world. No one knows how many individuals are multilingual, but, for example, in Ghana and Nigeria, which have single official languages, "as many as 90% of the population may be regularly using more than one language" (Crystal 1987:360). Code switching from one language to another, and even language mixing, within utterances are very common in multilingual communities. In addition to the five thousand or so native languages, many people also speak a second language which has special properties and is no one's native language. Such pidgin languages are remarkably similar in structure even when their speakers have had no contact. Pidgins may be short-lived until conditions change, or they may change and grow into full-use languages (Hancock 1971). Because of the concern over the negative effects of pidgin language on deaf children and the proposals for bilingual education, these issues are worthy of consideration in some depth. Some clarifications of international multilin-gualism, code switching, pidgins and creoles, and the relation between different language situations and language acquisition are necessary to objective consideration of the language planning efforts being proposed in the education of deaf children.

Multilingualism

Various models of multilingualism occur in the world (See e.g. Stewart 1968, Grosjean 1982). Language contact may lead to assimilation, acculturation, or preservation; i.e. the languages may all be preserved, one or more may disappear, or the languages may be preserved but be used differently from before (restricted to home use but not school, and so forth). Sometimes two varieties of the same language or different languages under clearly delimited conditions are separated by social values (diglossia). One has high prestige and one low prestige as a colloquial variety. Literature standardization and a strong tradition of grammatical study will be conducted in the high prestige variety, which is usually said to be more complex grammatically and learned through formal education. There is not a continuum of high to low language but a sharp delimitation. The deaf community was long thought to be a diglossic situation (Stokoe 1970), but observations of a more complex set of sociolinguistic variables (e.g. Erting 1983) have led many to doubt that the demarcation between English and ASL is at all sharp (Lee 1982). ASL and English are different languages, sign and speech are different modes. It is easy to see how the modes would be mixed on a continuum—one can sign English or speak ASL or sign and speak simultaneously.

Talking about a *language* continuum has been less comfortable. Some models have placed ASL at one end, English at the other, and PSE (pidgin) in the center of the continuum. This model, though, preserves a discredited notion of a pidgin as a mixture of languages. Yet there is language mixing in this community, and mixing is recommended by some as a language strategy for school teachers (e.g. Strong & Charlson 1989). The relative prestige status of the two languages within the deaf community and the hearing community surrounding them has also shifted somewhat in the last twenty years, so that ASL enjoys more prestige than it once did and is the subject of a movement to preserve and enhance it.

It is worthwhile to distinguish between bilingual or multilingual communities and individuals. Language has different roles to play within a speech community (even a monolingual community has multiple speech styles). Language is not just grammar and vocabulary. Communicative competence includes principles of usage as well as principles of grammar. In many bilingual communities, only rare individuals are themselves bilingual. In others, individual bilingualism is the norm. There are also different common patterns of individual bilingualism. Early researchers (Weinreich 1953, Ervin and Osgood 1954) distinguished three types of bilinguals: (1) coordinate bilinguals have two separate language systems, acquired in separate contexts; (2) compound bilinguals merge their two languages at the conceptual level; (3) subordinate bilinguals rapidly translate a fluent second language through a dominant language. The two languages can be learned sequentially: one language is learned as the native one and then the second one is learned; or simultaneously: both languages are learned as native from different sources (e.g from parents and nanny or mother and father).

Although Weinreich's categories fell into discredit, both because of the results of further research and because the theory was oversimplified, some attraction to the schema of these three types of bilingualism remains for some theorists (Appel & Muysken 1987). A revision takes into account a continuum between coordinate and com-pound bilingualism and a mixed division of components; e.g. one may be compound bilingual for vocabulary and coordinate for grammar. However the languages are organized for an individual, they must be kept separate for interaction with monolinguals. Macnamara (1967) hypothesized a set of switches to control the languages, but Paradis (1977) stresses that using a language appropriately is like other linguistic choices people make, based on context. Probably no "switch" is necessary if we consider the kinds of adaptations people make in different contexts (interlocutor, situation, topic, etc.). There may be a common cognitive, academic, proficiency that underlies both languages that a bilingual individual speaks and that transfers from one language to the other (Cummins 1980, 1984). This underlying conceptual knowledge is different from surface fluency needed for basic interpersonal skills

(Cummins 1980, Skutnabb-Kangas 1983), suggesting that the ability to select the appropriate register (literacy-based and cognitively demanding vs. interpersonal and highly context-bound) is as crucial to successful communication as the selection of a grammatical rule or the language *per se*. Nevertheless, we do not yet have good understanding of the ways that individuals organize two languages. The implication for language curriculum would be to use communication rather than (or in addition to) language as an organizing principle and to develop two foci through the life span: (1) interpersonal communi-cation would focus on the surface fluency (signs, print, and speech) needed for face-to-face interaction in a range of dyadic and small group relationships; and (2) literate communication would focus on reading and writing in education but also on the development of higher cognitive skills (using signs, print, and speech) associated with a literate, education-oriented culture (Wells 1989).

The concern is practical as well as theoretical. There is considerable fear among many that children exposed to two languages will master neither one, as if there is only so much language space available which is in danger of being split between the languages, leaving both inadequately developed. The notion of *semilingualism* receives some support from language tests, analysis of spoken samples, and the impressions of parents (Appel & Muysken 1987).

"Bilingual children are not able to use all the morphological devices their monolingual age-mates use" (Appel and Muysken 1987: 108). Or their vocabulary or verbal test scores and ideational fluency may be inferior (Paradis 1978, 1980, 1981, Krashen, Scarcella & Long 1982). No differences, however, show up on nonverbal intelligence tests (Paradis 1978, 1981), and there are some intellectual advantages in flexibility and abstractness and in code-switching abilities (Appel & Muysken 1987). It is unclear whether semilingualism is really a deficit or a pejorative characterization of a difference.

Whether the difference is due to actual differences brought on by the children's bilingualism or on test factors and the "marginal man syndrome" is hotly debated. The differences appear minor, nevertheless. The differences that show in statistics on ethnic groups are often claimed to be the result not of language background but of acceptance and other social factors. Thus we have little guidance on determining whether deaf children raised as simultaneous or sequential bilinguals will have an advantage or suffer. Certainly, my work on Alice (Maxwell 1983a) if stopped early would have indicated a disadvantage from a mixed and simultaneous situation, but studies of her at age 8 show no disadvantage, her achievement at grade level, and an interest in communicating widely.

Pidgins & creoles

As an alternative to widespread individual bilingualism of native languages, language contact may lead to the development of a pidgin. According to one view, pidgins are languages that have "mixed" lexicons but are genuine languages in their own right. According to another view, pidgins result from the use of simplified registers and broken languages in the same communication situation and are thus less stable and autonomous than 'languages' (See Valdman 1977 and others). A third view places pidgins closer to innate or universal language properties in the brain (Bickerton 1974, 1977). Sometimes the sign language literature sounds as if "pidgin" is some sort of pejorative, but pidgins are not just poorly learned or corrupted forms of some standard language. Typically a pidgin is a contact vernacular, not a native language, used between speakers who have no other language in common. Thus it has been applied (e.g. Woodward 1973, Reilly & McIntire 1980) to communication between deaf and hearing people, as between users of ASL and users of English who do not share each other's language. Recently this characterization has been questioned (Cokely 1983, Maxwell & Bernstein 1985, Bochner & Albertini 1988, Lucas & Valli 1989). Certainly it seems reasonable to imagine (although there are no studies of these individuals) that there are deaf people who use ASL and who know no English and hearing people who use signs but know no ASL, except for some shared lexical signs. The more typical situation is that deaf persons who use ASL have also been exposed to English since early childhood.

Pidgins are typically limited to certain functions, such as trading or housekeeping or some other economic activity. People develop pidgins in contact with members of another group. It makes sense to talk of a pidgin continuum, to the extent that the source languages are still used, and pidgin speakers will use more or less of the rules of their own first language within their use of pidgin. A creole is usually considered a native language of most of its speakers: a language learned in the home with lexicon and syntax sufficient for meeting all the communication needs of its speakers. One particular quality of a creole is minimization of redundancy in its grammar; older languages typically have a great deal of grammatical redundancy. Creoles are typically inferior in social but not linguistic status; they are just young. Even English could be classified as a creole because of its incorporation of Middle English, French, African languages, Spanish, etc., especially American English; but English has been a language for hundreds of years and English speaking governments have a lot of money and weapons, and there are a lot of books printed in English, so English is considered a language not a creole.

Pidgins & language acquisition

The origins of pidgins and creoles are highly controversial. Three theories are frequently advanced, but there is little clear evidence to help us choose between them. We haven't watched enough pidgins and creoles in the act of arising. We are left with choosing on logical grounds. Which is more likely: replacement of the lexicon, convergent structural development, or language universals? These ideas are important to the student of deaf individuals' language, because they relate to language acquisition.

One theory (monogenetic? "the traveling salesman theory") was based on the travels of Portuguese sailor-traders. The idea was that they went to so many places that they influenced the development of pidgins all over the world. In modern times, of course, we have observed similar pidgins where the Portuguese never ventured.

The polygenetic—spontaneous generation—theory posits that a pidgin arises during relatively casual, short-term contact between groups that do not have a language in common (no single salesman). If interlingual contact is long and institutionalized, then the pidgin becomes fixed, expanded, and diffused, and it becomes appropriate to call it a creole. There may be no intermarriage and everybody may keep her native language. The creole thus becomes a lingua franca that everyone can use. Sometimes one language is chosen as a lingua franca, the way that

pilots all have to learn English for aircraft control, and
sometimes the lingua franca is a development from a
pidgin. A few pidgins are quite stable, perhaps
because social conditions prevent full–scale learning
of second languages fluently; they keep the distinct
language groups in limited contact over time and
cause recognition of the pidgin as a separate entity
needed as a lingua franca.

In other cases pidgin communities abandon the
original languages. In this view, pidgins become
creoles through children, as pidgin speakers marry or
settle together. Suppose your mother was a Hindi
speaker and your father a Zulu speaker, but they both
also spoke trade pidgin. When they got married, they
found that lots of other couples in the neighborhood
were mixed, too; so instead of using one spouse's
language or the other, they just kept speaking pidgin
for everything. When you were born, they spoke
pidgin to you instead of Hindi or Zulu, so you don't
know anything but pidgin. For *you* it's not a pidgin
language for limited purposes, it's your native
language. As your family spoke pidgin for
everything, the pidgin got more developed and
elaborated. Since everybody in the neighborhood was
doing essentially the same thing, the community
became a pidgin-speaking community. Eventually,
only the old people knew anything but pidgin, and as
they died off, the community had only one language.
This definition of pidgin sounds as if you dump both

languages in a barrel and mix them up, picking some features from each and some other features that are in neither, but sometimes the mixing isn't balanced. When people settle together, it may be that *relexification* occurs, rapid replacement of vocabulary of a language by lexical items taken from another language. For example, on a border, speakers might keep Spanish structure but adopt English vocabulary (resulting in a kind of language mixing that is often ridiculed by speakers living in the interior).

A quite different theory posits that pidgins and creoles share features that constitute linguistic universals (Kay & Sankoff 1974). There has been a lot of debate about what aspects of language might be innate (or hard-wired). It may be that pidgins and creoles are windows into the brain, and that when people do not share a language, innate linguistic principles take over (Bickerton 1974, 1977). If pidgin languages are impossible native languages, because the rules are insufficiently elaborated; e.g. distinctions are vague between action and state or between assertion and presupposition (Traugott 1977), then individuals fall back on their innate "pre-wiring" for language and combine this knowledge with categorizing of what they do perceive in the language environment, however mixed or ill-understood it may be. Creolization, in this view, consequently goes beyond pidginization and results in a combination of innate principles, inferred structures, and elaboration and restructuring, as the system of communication grows in number of speakers and in functions. Creoles tend to develop complex embeddings and morphological structures, even cliticization of adverbs and particles (Sankoff & Laberge 1973). Traugott argues that many changes are due to the natural phonological processes that support fluent cohesion.

> Since pidgins tend to be spoken slowly and somewhat unrhythmically, the force of the phonological processes cannot be expected to be very great in pidgins. In creoles, however, they can have considerably greater importance since, like other native languages, creoles are spoken with speed and fluency. (Traugott 1977: 87)

Quigley and various colleagues have pointed out similarities and differences between the English sentence structure development (in written form) of hearing impaired students and that of hearing native children and of hearing foreigners learning English as a second language (Quigley & King 1980). To what extent do reports of poor bimodal communication by hearing parents and teachers represent a stage on a continuum of sign learning by those parents and teachers? It is possible that they represent some sort of broken language or foreigner talk of persons who have imperfectly learned a new language. This assumption seems implicit in the studies whose conclusions call for greater training and have little or nothing to do with bimodality *per se* any more than pronunciation of second language learners of English have to do with the study of English phonology.

Speakers of broken language can be ranked along a continuum representing various stages of the language acquisition process; seen thus pidginization is an unstable result of variable learning (Ferguson & DeBose 1977)

Pidgins & signed languages

How might these theories relate to sign-speech bimodality? The first theory—the traveling salesman (minus the Portuguese sailor)—would allow for the reasonableness of the idea that ASL vocabulary might relexicalize English, so that there truly is a combination of the two languages, that replaces English vocabulary and is planted in English structure. Whether that succeeds or not depends on resistance, and there is a great deal of resistance from preservers of ASL, but also a great deal of acceptance in practice There is also some lexicalization of English words into ASL so that native signers see the use of mouthing as a part of ASL (Davis 1989). The second theory would suggest that there may indeed be a pidgin or creole used commonly for deaf–hearing interaction, and that it is neither a representation of English nor a combination *per se* of the two languages but is a special language to be found in that situation. While many have claimed that this is so, few studies make it clear what situations and conditions they may actually be capturing. How does this situation relate to residential schools, where hearing teachers are in the majority in structured classroom situations with deaf children, and deaf adults are in the majority in unstructured situations with deaf children? Erting (1985 a,b) pointed out some of the variation in language that can be found in schools for the deaf. We need to know more about the variation and the sociolinguistic variables that might predict it.

The third theory suggests that the language actually produced in spontaneous deaf-hearing interactions, or the language of deaf children without fluent input, may contain language primitives that reveal the universals of the brain. The data from fluent SC users certainly does not fit this description, but other data might. Children may be a different story. The adults in our studies had experience with both ASL and English, but deaf children's language products, based on input of various kinds, may reveal a complex interplay of linguistic universals balanced with the learning of units of language they have heard or seen and their own inferences about underlying organization. Both hearing second language learners and deaf children sometimes embed learned units into original sentences; e.g. "May I want some water." Longitudinal studies investigating this premise would be highly welcome. If children are receiving variable and broken input of several kinds and falling back on their innate abilities, combining these with inferences from the input and with some learned units, is it any wonder that the sequence of acquisition does not exactly parallel that of monolingual hearing children or second language learning adults? Careful longitudinal studies of children should consider these various models, instead of measuring the deaf child's language against hearing norms. *After all these years of concern over the deaf child's acquisition of language, we know next to nothing about how it proceeds.* [Editor's emphasis]

Critics often focus on the claim that deaf children are not receiving "good" input in one language and thus are creating pidgins. Perhaps we should ask if this is necessarily bad or even, if it is bad, whether it is likely to continue. We might discover what sorts of practices could take this into account and so enhance the children's ability to converge on conventional language. Perhaps deaf children born to hearing parents will have a path to conventional language that is different from the native language acquisition of other children, but a path that might still lead to fluency. Analysis of deaf children's language for assessment purposes presents problems. We can test children, or count features and structures, of ASL and English, of course. Taking a language sample, however, a standard step recommended by teachers of the deaf and speech or language pathologists, poses a challenge: what are the grounds of evaluation? Asked another way, what language, or languages, should be the basis for the assessment? It seems that fluency at some end point is more important than orthodoxy at the beginning point Therefore we might keep a mind more open to the language of young deaf children—in addition to counting English structures, we might study several children over time to map their progress and seek patterns that may be shared by many deaf children.

ASL, pidgin, & English

But how can children learn English (or ASL) if there is such a mixture of input and so much of the input is substandard? It is worthwhile to consider aspects of relations between spoken languages. What is the relation between language contact and language interference? If we look around the world to places where languages are in contact (at borders, between ethnic groups, minority language enclaves in standard language communities, and so forth), we find that there is not one inevitable outcome for all situations. It is neither inevitable that bilingualism will obtain nor that one language will disappear. The possible outcomes are several:

1.There might be a perfect shift from one language to another with extinction of the first—ASL might disappear or English might never be used by deaf signers for communication There might be abrupt creolization in which only the vocabulary of the second language is acquired, a process similar to relexification. Thus there might be signs in use but no

ASL grammar. Something like this happened in the Caribbean, where there was no interim pidgin stage. If that pattern took place, some kind of MCE might be the language used by all the deaf, with no ASL structure surviving as older people died. This scenario seems to be feared by many who cherish ASL.

2.Both languages might be maintained, with light to heavy interference found in borrowing—ASL and spoken English would both be used, English speakers would use many ASL expressions, and ASL users would use much English. They would probably switch from one to the other in talk, but they would be able to talk to monolinguals in both languages as well.

3.Another possibility is what linguists call *Sprachbund*, an area in which genetic heterogeneity is gradually replaced by typological homo-geneity (Jakobson 1958): only those elements of structure are accepted by one language from another language that correspond to its own tendencies of development. So one's own language is maintained for communication with one's own group, yet there is also frequent communication across groups and some incorporation of the other language where the two happen to coincide. The Deaf would use ASL with each other and the hearing would use spoken English with each other; deaf individuals would use some speech and signed English with the hearing, and hearing individuals would use some ASL, but pidginization would stop. The lines between the languages actually become firmer and the languages actually become less open to borrowing.

4. There might be jargonization of the minority language, in which only vocabulary is maintained; e.g. Gypsy Spanish or Anglo-Romany. If that happened ASL vocabulary alone would be maintained, but no one would use its grammar or any regular grammar.

5.Or the most variegated result might occur, a postcreole community, like Jamaica or Hawaii, in which there is a great deal of dialect variation, especially in vocabulary. There is a socioeconomically oriented ctinuum of speech varieties, with a large number of intermediate varieties. The two extremes are mutually intelligible, but each speaker commands a span of this continuum and is capable of making adjustments up or down, depending on interlocutor and audience. This last occurs most often when the dominant official language is the same as the creole vocabulary base and when the social system provides for social mobility (and sufficient corrective pressures from schools, etc). If decreolization takes place, then the creole becomes gradually more similar to the standard language of its lexical base. Thus we would continue to see a continuum of signing and bimodal varieties between signed English (of some representation pattern) and ASL, since the vocabulary base is shared. If deaf individuals moved toward more use of English signs, then decreolization would lead to widespread use of signed English and diminished use of ASL.

Studies of some young deaf children (Livingston 1983, Gee & Goodhart 1985, S. Supalla 1986) suggest that in spite of manually coded English input, the language the children produce has more similarity to ASL than to English. Whether this is because the children are actually exposed to forms like ASL or because the language they express as a part of learning coincidentally resembles ASL (because of language universals, visual structure, or cognitive constraints) is not clear at this time. Fischer (1978) suggested that ASL is recreolized with each generation because of the influx of new speakers and the scarcity of input. Such constant linguistic activity by new speech community members would undermine the tendency toward decreolization and full blown life as a stable language. Other deaf individuals, however, do use English (Maxwell 1983a, Lucas & Valli 1989), although the features of English represented may not be those of the invented sign systems.

Researchers have begun to recognize variation among signers. One of the first dimensions noted of variation in the sign language community was variation between deaf-deaf and deaf-hearing dyadic communicators (e.g. Gee & Goodhart 1984). Within the deaf popu-lation, differences in language use have been associated with age of entry and parental language (e.g. Mayberry & Tuchman 1983, Reilly, McIntire & Bellugi in press), geographic regions (Stokoe, Casterline & Croneberg 1965), ethnicity (Woodward 1976, Maxwell & Smith-Todd 1986, Aramburo 1989, Johnson & Erting 1989,), and sex (Nowell 1989). The social stigma attached by many deaf and hearing individuals alike to the invented sign systems (Lucas & Valli 1989) seems to have prevented many researchers from examining signed features of English and acknowledging that many deaf individuals are fluent in English and value their fluency (in speech or in sign, as well as writing). Nevertheless, not everyone who signs some features of English is fully fluent in English or in representing spoken fluent English (e.g. Lucas & Valli 1989). The extent to which pidginization and code mixing are taking place apparently varies from speaker to speaker, with many idiosyncrasies.

Lee (1983) and Lucas and Valli (1989) point out some of the code-mixing features of some adult signed language, and Maxwell (1983a) points out some of the code-mixing features of one deaf child's signed and spoken language. The former also mention the notion that members of the deaf signing community have a wide variety of individual grammars. Indeed, the model of language variation that includes a great deal of idiosyncrasy and that, unlike the notion of a trade or limited pidgin, includes plenty of access to target native languages is not a multilingual or a pidgin contact model as much as it is a postcreole model.

In a postcreole situation, variation in language is not based strictly on broad sociological categories nor on separate language communities. Significant language variation is not explained by social stratification, ethnicity, or parental language. A factor of great importance is individual psychological identity (Le Page & Tabouret-Keller 1985, Bain 1983). In other words, a mixture of languages and language features is available, but for reasons of psychological identity, individuals exhibit considerable idiosyncrasy in their language. Jamaica is said to be such a postcreole community, in which a classroom of children from the same neighborhood may reveal a number of idiosyncratic grammars and speech choices (Le Page & Tabouret-Keller 1985). Although for different historical reasons, the situation of deaf signers in the United States also provides a variety of language models to deaf children in one community, and observations of children in classes of deaf children suggest that there will be children exposed to little fluent language of any kind and children exposed to more than one model of fluent language. The community is subject to constant reshuffling because of population entry and school pressures, and the variety of language and life backgrounds keeps shifting the language available. Within one community are a deaf individual who gestures vaguely, using some ASL signs but little fluent grammar, a deaf individual who signs and mouths simultaneous English morphemes, a deaf individual who signs ASL fluently and sometimes uses code mixing with non-ASL signers, etc. Creoles develop in situations where there is relatively little identification by adults with the pidgin, because it is not their native language. Therefore, first generation creole speakers are presumably subject to relatively little suppressive judgment by older speakers. Unusually numerous experiments with language may thus survive, since there is minimal need to create "cover-up" rules to accommodate oneself to the speech patterns of one's own class—though systematic variation certainly does develop, given the needs of communicating with members of other classes. That the structural elaborations developing in the creolization process do not generalize very fast, at least in some creole situations, and do not proceed in steps as predictable as those of first language acquisition, would seem to be explained by the absence of a native language model, and "the social distance" from the superstrate language or languages (Traugott 1977: 87-88).

Certainly in the case of deaf children, there is enormous "suppressive judgment from older speakers" of English and considerable effort expended to get the child to accommodate to the superstrate language. Creolization may occur because the children have little perceptual access to fluent English, but that is not for want of concern on the part of adults. Le Page and Tabouret-Keller (1985) stress that a postcreole continuum of code-mixing and idiosyn-cratic grammars are related to identity (e.g. greater use of Spanish pronunciation and sentence structure indicates greater identification with Spanish elements of the culture) and can lead to great variety in a group of children exposed to essentially the same background in a postcreole situation. One feature of adolescence in residential schools may be suppressive judgment to accommodate to ASL, contributing to an identity challenge.

What will happen in deaf education?

Which scenario seems most likely for deaf education? Will ASL disappear or is there enough political meaning for it to continue? What effect has mainstreaming had on ASL? Is a stable bilingual situation likely? Are deaf people likely to be universally bilingual? Are hearing people in deaf education likely to be bilingual in the future?

Because of the limitations profound deafness places on learning a spoken language, deaf persons are unlikely to abandon signs and speak only English. Because it is a minority language, hearing persons in large numbers are not likely to become fluent in ASL. Thus interaction between ASL signing deaf persons and English speaking hearing persons is likely to continue rather than disappear. Because deaf children begin signing at different ages and only rarely are born to fluent signing adults (whether ASL or MCE), there is likely to be a great deal of broken language in the environment. Adults will use both broken ASL and broken MCE of varying degrees of intelligibility. Children exposed to odd and varying input may reflect much of this oddness in their communication. The presence of more than half the deaf schoolchildren in public schools (*American Annals of the Deaf Directory* 1988) rather than in residential schools suggests even more strongly that there will be high numbers of broken language users available.

The average length of time of a teacher in the profession is three years (Corbett & Jensema 1981), which is hardly long enough to achieve fluency in bimodal communication or ASL, given how little instruction usually precedes employment (Maxwell 1985). Since the adult deaf persons who could provide sign language input are not employed in the public schools (though they are present in the residential school), it is hard to imagine that sign language fluency will be common in the public schools, especially fluency in ASL On the other hand, if teacher proficiency tests become common elements of certification *and* if deaf individuals are involved in these evaluations, hearing fluency in ASL may improve.

The preponderance of hearing authority figures fluent in English but not in bimodality, and probably largely ignorant of ASL, seems like a "perfect" environment for the persistence of unstable broken language, or even for the jargonization of ASL. That is, many deaf children and hearing adults might use ASL and MCE vocabulary without any regular grammar—with a semantic structure but no grammatical structure. It is worthwhile to remember that pidgins typically arise from situations where the input languages are fluent but the output is reduced and different. If there is no fluent sign input either from ASL signers or from fluent bimodal communicators, the situation seems ripe for the jargonization of sign. On the other hand, there is a small movement to establish the teaching of ASL as a foreign language in the nation's high schools (e.g. in California and Texas).[1] If this movement grows, it may help maintain ASL The presence of formal pedagogic means of learning may confer enhanced prestige on the language, and encourage the sort of self-monitoring that leads to standardization and "upgrading" (Ferguson & DeBose 1977:118) among deaf and hearing signers alike. Besides, ASL just may persist because enough people want it to.

[1]See also SLS 59 (1988).

A systematic study of linguistic change in the last twenty years would help us judge how ASL has been affected by the MCE movement, how ASL constraints have affected the acceptance and use of the various MCE systems, and could help us predict the future of both on linguistic grounds. A study of the various social and political dimensions of the situation might help us to predict whether ASL is about to take over as the language of instruction (but who will teach? only deaf teachers? what will parents learn? what about reading?) or whether MCE and/or bimodality are about to be repudiated generally. Because of the difficulty that most deaf children have acquiring fluency in spoken English, it seems safe to predict that most children will continue to use some form of signs. Will the signs be part of bimodal English, pidgin, ASL, or all three?

Proposals

This brings us to a closer examination of some of the more recent proposals offered in this area. With the preceding discussion as background, it should be clear why caution is warranted. Issues such as the nature of language, communication, and language acquisition; the definition of linguistic pidgins and other codes; the nature of bilingual education; and political-pedagogical agendas all become crucial to this discussion.

Training proposals: One problem with evaluating simultaneous communication or manually coded English (usually employing a system such as SEE$_2$) is that is it currently impossible to separate poor implementation from the idea itself; i.e. it might be failing because people haven't been properly trained, etc. If teachers and parents lack sufficient skills, then, practically speaking, MCE/SC cannot accomplish what it is supposed to do. The possibility is that MCE/SC, in whatever specific form selected, might be more effective and successful if teachers and parents were better trained in its performance. This is a position that might be exemplified by the work Swisher (1983, 1984, Swisher & Thompson 1985). A related point is the plethora of different systems and partial systems in place People often bewail the lack of standardization and uniformity from region to region, indeed from classroom to classroom.

As discussed earlier, the issue of more effective training is one highly influenced by the political and pedagogical agenda and one's beliefs regarding the necessary conditions for language acquisition. If one believes that the purpose of simultaneous communication is to represent fully and exactly the structure of the English spoken, and that the availability of such sign input is critical to English language acquisition in deaf children, then this training solution would hold great attraction.

To date, the discussion has been focused almost exclusively on the morphological level of fit between speech and sign. We would like to see more research on other levels, so that a decision to improve training could achieve consensus about the level of fit that is the goal of training, and so that the practitioners would be more aware of what is lost or distorted and could make decisions about how to teach those aspects of language. For example, to pose a radical idea, perhaps one might decide that inflectional fit (e.g. use of a suffix like -ed or -s) is the *least* likely to be close, because of performance factors. Then instruction would have to take into account that children are exposed comfortably and fluently to other levels of English but not to inflectional morphemes; it would then make sense to investigate whether inflectional morphemes could be taught through other means, such as writing. (It is worth noting here that English inflectional morphemes pose a problem for deaf children in all educational situations.)

Modification proposals: In discussing modifications of simultaneous communication, questions regarding nomenclature become important. It is hard to know whether pidgin is being recommended or whether a recommendation is being made for recognition of some other inter-mediate learning variety. It is also crucially important to consider differences in children, in adults communicating with them, in situations, in the use of vocal language, and other such factors before we slap a label on some language variety and misrepresent the learning and communicating processes of some child.

It has been suggested by numerous researchers that the mandate to represent *exactly* the structure of spoken English in simultaneous signs may be unrealistic on linguistic, psychological, and social grounds (obviously thinking of the fit at the morphological and word level). It may also be undesirable if the effort to do so interferes with the natural flow of communication (i.e. with the fit at the message and discourse levels and with the motivation to communicate). And it has been suggested that for purposes of language acquisition the exact representation of English morphological structure may not be as critical as once thought. What aspects of language are present in early input and how are they conveyed? Various proposals for solutions in this vein can be inferred from some of the literature, although these have not always been explicitly made by individual writers.

In a survey of TC teachers across the country, Woodward and Allen (1987) discovered that teachers who report that they are using a Signed English system also report that they use a great many ASL features in their communication. One explicit discussion of various strategies that teachers apply (Strong & Charlson 1989) notes that these are all represented in teacher practices. Proposals have included: (1) teachers and parents should drop the use of the various invented sign markers for English morphology (i.e. move from a one morpheme to one sign correspondence to a one word to one sign correspondence); (2) simultaneous communicators should not attempt to speak along with their signing (i.e. reduce the psycholinguistic processing needs); (3) simultaneous communicators should incorporate more ASL features in their signing (i.e. deliberately mix the languages, leading to questions of maintenance of the two languages as separate, to pidginization, or to language mixing); and (4) simultaneous communi-cators should just do "what comes naturally"— which relies on fluency and which may not be so much a conscious effort to represent the spoken English manually as an effort to communicate *bimodally* (which is quite a different matter). Examination of doing "what comes naturally" might reveal com-municative values as yet unexamined.

*Bilingual ASL/English proposals:*Issues of bilingualism certainly include political and pedagogical issues, and the question of nomenclature. Reasonable motivations for enhancing the place of ASL in pedagogy include respect for the symbolic meaning of ASL, for the deaf as a political and social group, interest in using a language that is naturally adapted to the visual mode and that is obviously learnable, and learning a language that has a history with meaning for deaf people. Language is intimately related to identity,[1] and so favoring of ASL in pedagogy is intimately connected with whether one is able to see the deaf as a handicapped group lagging behind but assimilable or able to see the deaf as a social group with some separatism.

While everyone admits the desirability of American deaf children's learning English, some have explored the possibility of a larger role for ASL in the communicative development of deaf children by proposing a bilingual approach to their education. Recent versions of such a suggestion have been made by Akamatsu & Stewart (1987), Luetke-Stahlman (1983), and Strong (1988). These proposals might employ team teaching, with ASL signed by a deaf native and English spoken by a hearing native, with deaf educators working in sign language and hearing educators working in spoken and written English. This approach emphasizes that the adults need to coordinate their teaching and coordinate their language use so that children have clear and separate models of the two languages and the two modes. Children themselves may produce simultaneous signed and spoken language as they learn to sort through their languages and their modes, but adults

---

[1] See Mottez, "Deaf Identity," in SLS 68.

do not. Thus the children can identify with both deaf adults and with hearing parents and the larger hearing community. Generally this type of proposal involves the use of both ASL and some form of English-based simultaneous communication throughout the school day. This might be either formally scheduled or arranged, as in Strong's model; or it might be more free-flowing, based on social and instructional circumstances. The idea would be that deaf children can develop as bilingual (ASL-English) individuals by being bilingual throughout their development. Experiments in France (Bouvet 1982, 1983) and Sweden (McConnell 1989) offer models of bilingual education.

The ESL proposal: This is a proposal to employ ASL exclusively for all functions, starting with the early years. Based on the recognition that the best method for learning any language is interaction with a fluent language-using caregiver in the early years, such proposals include recommendations for day care employing ASL-using deaf adults. If education is conducted in ASL, the reasoning goes, then deaf children will have adequate opportunity to acquire a language naturally to the level of fluency while they are yet young. Another aspect of the recommendation is the belief that if children are taught in ASL, then they will not fall behind cognitively or in skills and information. English would then be taught as a second language through formal instruction, and it would be taught only after fluency in ASL had been acquired. This proposal names ASL as the native language, with English to be taught as a second language, and it has recently been associated with the Gallaudet University Linguistics Department (Johnson et al. 1989). They find no value whatever in attempts to use simultaneous communication and would suppress it. They propose that deaf children be raised in an ASL environment from earliest childhood, so that ASL develops as their first language. English would be introduced later on during the elementary school years, and taught as a *second* language.

One type of evidence that deaf children approach English as a second language now is offered by Quigley and King (1980), who compared the written English structures of deaf children with foreign learners of English as a second language. Readers also perceive such writing as similar (Langston & Maxwell 1988). There has lately been some interest in the interference of ASL on English writing, as a means of understanding the writing better and as demonstration that it makes sense to consider ASL the native language of deaf children and English a second language anyway.

While this proposal is primarily concerned with raising the status of ASL in education, the teaching of English has been little addressed within it. The fact is that the methods of teaching English as a second language are rarely successful with hearing people without other major implementations. Not least of the problems of second language instruction is the need to provide for functionality of the target language. Language has a number of functions, and learning a language cannot be restricted to one or a partial function if its success is to be likely (Titone 1983). The integrative function of language is to establish the status of its speakers as members of a group. The expressive function is to display one's linguistic skills. The communicative function is to transmit denotative referential information. And then there is literacy and the higher level cognition based on language. Pidginization occurs as a function of incomplete learning when a language is restricted to its communicative function and is not used for integrative or expressive functions. Whether a potential second language learner accomplishes that learning or not is related to factors of social distance: language shock (inability to name things leads to shame), culture shock (problem solving skills fail), culture stress (centers around questions of identity, underemployment, prejudice, etc). Where social and psychological distance prevail, lack of fluency will persist in the speech of second language learners (Schumann 1978). According to this view, where social and psychological distance prevail between deaf and hearing people, and where learning is restricted in English, it is likely that pidginization rather than fluent English will persist.

Thus, if nothing is done about the conditions of English learning, it seems highly unlikely that English will be learned any better under this situation than under the current conditions. English, and especially speech, carry such ambiguous values for deaf individuals today (Nash & Nash 1981, Kannapell 1989, Maxwell & Kraemer in press) that language learning is not just a matter of skills. What might be achieved is better education through ASL, of course, and educators and families might be willing to trade that possibility for the risk of maintenance of weak English. After all, the argument might go, they're aren't learning English or much else now.

Conclusions

All of these proposals reflect the desire to impose a structure on the community that simply is not there now. To suggest that a monolingual community become bilingual would be one thing, but how likely is it that a community (in which various individuals code-mix, use one language, or support bilingualism) will eliminate the code-mixing and simply switch to prominence the language that has been repressed (it used to be ASL; henceforth it will be English)? How likely is it that parents who are native English speakers are going to abandon their language in favor of ASL and wait several years before wanting their children to use their language? Can they be influenced to accept this proposal? It seems to have the most passion right now.

The widespread concern with the use of MCE systems may fuel the sort of radical change many are advocating. The modification proposals seem to require the least change in that they want to supplant (in different ways) artificial processes with naturally occurring code-mixing ones. Battles constantly range over classroom behavior. For the community at large, at present, there is no evidence of a coming change in code-mixing, in ASL, in English representation such as found in a postcreole situation, or considerable individual variation. There seems little evidence or reasonable conjecture that ASL will edge out English as a goal of education, given the desirability of learning English in the U.S. and the amount of exposure deaf individuals have to English in their education and daily lives. There seems little reason to expect that ASL will disappear, either, given the commitment of so many to its value and its importance to Deaf identity.

Bimodality and code–mixing are useful and prevalent in the community. Given the importance of these language varieties to individual identity and the multiplicity of available adjustments in representation, grammar, and mode, it seems likely that grammars will be idiosyncratic reflecting different orientations to identity. A program of investigation of actual language use by deaf individuals and between deaf and hearing individuals must become more descriptive and allow of such a possibility without an *a priori* negative bias. As far as education should be concerned, there might well be reason to appreciate children's varied communication and varied identities in interpersonal com-munication. Education might acknowledge such a variable commun-icative situation and abandon the desire for a single "hearing" or "Deaf" monolingual or bilingual standard; it might focus instead on a standard of situational appropriateness for inter-personal communication with different individuals, in different situations, etc. It might strive for literate skills and values demanding higher level cognition.

Instead of presenting conclusions here, a few commencements are in order. We are at the beginning of understanding what's going on with deaf children, teachers, and parents. The sign situation appears much more varied and complex than we once thought. Writers must describe as well as label and define. Variation and different models of languages in society (pidgins, creoles, learner languages, multilingual speech communities, postcreole communities, etc.) need to be part of teachers' knowledge if teachers are to be consumers and critics of research that uses such models. We need to understand more about the sociopolitical dimensions of languages in the Deaf Community, the families of deaf children, and the professionals who work with them all. And, not least, we need more description of language varieties and language interaction (including comprehension).

How can we choose among models of the community and proposals for educational policy on the basis of so little data? Almost every time a researcher (including the writer) collects new data or tries a new analysis, there's a new suggestion for the "right" way to interpret the situation. Schools can't stand still while kids keep growing. Consequently, educational policy controversies and uncontrolled experiments will always be ahead of data based research. It does seem that we might approach *data based studies* with open minds to think through the implications of different theories.

REFERENCES

Akamatsu, C.& D. Stewart
  1987 A model program for training teachers of the deaf, *American Annals of the Deaf* 132, 366-372.
American Annals of the Deaf, DirectoryIssue 1988

Anthony, D.
  1971 *Seeing Essential English.* Anaheim, CA: Anaheim Union School District.
Appel, R. & P. Muysken
  1987 *Language Contact & Bilingualism.* London: Edward Arnold.

Aramburo, A.
    1989 Sociolinguistic aspect of the black deaf community. In
    The Sociolinguistics of the Deaf Community, Lucas ed.
    San Diego: Academic Press.
Bain, B. (ed.)
    1983 *The Sociogenesis of Language & Human Conduct.* NY:
    Plenum.
Baker, C.
    1978 How does 'Sim-Com' fit into a bilingual approach to
    education?In *Proceedings of the 2nd NSSLRT*,
    Caccamise & Hicks eds. Silver Spring, MD: NAD.
- - - - -& D. Cokely
    1980 *American Sign Language: A Teacher's Resource Text
    on Grammar & Culture.* Silver Spring, MD: T. J.
    Publishers, Inc.
Baron, N.
    1981 *Speech, Writing & Sign.* Bloomington: Indiana U. Press.
Bellugi, U. & S. Fischer
    1972 A comparison of sign language & spoken language,
    Cognition 1, 173-200.
Bernstein, M., M. Maxwell &K. Matthews
    1985 Bimodal & bilingual communication in schools for the
    deaf, *Sign Language Studies*47, 127-140.
Bickerton, D.
    1974 Creolization, linguistic universals, natural semantax &
    the brain, *Working Papers in Linguistics*6, 125-140.
    1977 Pidginization & creolization. In *Pidgin & Creole
    Linguistics*, Valdman ed. Bloomington: Indiana U.P.
Bochner, J.& J. Albertini
    1988 Language varieties in the deaf population & their
    acquisition by children. In Strong 1988.

Bornstein, H.
  1975 *The Signed English Dictionary for Preschool &
     Elementary Levels*. Washington: Gallaudet Press.
- - - - - &K. Saulnier
  1981 Signed English: A brief follow-up to the first evaluation,
     American Annals of the Deaf 127, 69-72.
Bornstein, H. , K. Saulnier & L. Hamilton
  1980 Signed English: A first evaluation, *American Annals of
     the Deaf* 126, 467-481.
Bouvet, D.
  1982 *La parole de l'enfant sourd*. Paris: Presses
     Universitaires de France.
  1983 Bilingual education for deaf students. In *SLR '83*,
     Stokoe & Volterra eds. Silver Spring, MD: Linstok
     Press.
Brasel, K. & S. Quigley
  1977 Influence of certain language & communication
     environments in early childhood on the development of
     language in deaf individuals, *Journal of Speech &
     Hearing Research* 20, 95-107.
Bright, W.
  1982 Literature: Written & oral. In *Analyzing Discourse: Text
     & Talk*, Tannen ed. Washington: Georgetown U. Press.
Chomsky, N.
  1965 *Aspects of the Theory of Syntax*. The Hague: Mouton.
- - - - -& M. Halle
  1968 *The Sound Pattern of English*. NY: Harper & Row.
Cokely, D.
  1983 When is a pidgin not a pidgin:? An alternative analysis
     of the ASL-English contact situation, *Sign Language
     Studies* 38, 1-24.

Corbett, E. & C. Jensema
   1981 *Teachers of the Deaf: Descriptive Profiles.* Washington:
       Gallaudet College Press.
Crandall, K.
   1978 Inflectional morphemes in the manual English of young
       hearing-impaired children & their mothers, *Journal of
       Speech & Hearing Research*21, 372-386.Cross, T.
   1978 Mothers' speech & its association with the rate of
       linguistic development in young children. In *The
       Development of Communication,* Waterson & Snow
       eds. NY: John Wiley.
Crystal, D.
   1987 *The Cambridge Encyclopedia of Language.* London &
       NY: Cambridge University Press.
Cummins, J.
   1980 The construct of language proficiency in bilingual
       education. In*Current Issues in Bilingual Education,*
       Alaitis ed. Washington: Georgetown University Press.
   1984 *Bilingualism & Special Education.* Boston: Little, Brown.
Davis, J.
   1989 Distinguishing language contact phenomena in ASL
       interpretation. In Lucas ed. 1989.
Dewey, G.
   1971 *English Spelling: Roadblock to Reading.* NY: Columbia
       University Press.
Eagney, P.
   1987 ASL? English? Comparing comprehension, *American
       Annals ofThe Deaf*132, 272-275.
Erting, C.
   1983 Linguistic variation in a school for deaf children. In *SLR
       '83,* Stokoe & Volterra eds. Silver Spring, MD: Linstok
       Press.

1985a Cultural contact in a deaf classroom, *Anthropology & Education Quarterly*16, 225-243.

1985b Sociocultural dimensions of Deaf education, *Sign Language Studies*47, 111-126.

Ervin, S. & C. Osgood

1954 Second language learning & bilingualism. *Supplement , Journal of Abnormal & Social Psychology*49, 139-146.

Ferguson, C. & C. DeBose

1977 Simplified registers, broken language & pidginization. In *Pidgin & Creole Languages,*Valdman ed. Bloomington: Indiana University Press.

Fischer, S.

1978 Sign language & creoles. In *Understanding Language through Sign Language Research*, Siple ed. NY: Academic Press.

Gallagher, T. & H. Meador

1989 Communication mode use of two hearing-impaired adolescents in conversation, *Journal of Speech & Hearing Disorders*54, 570-575.

Gaustad, M.

1986 Longitudinal effects of manual English instruction on deaf children's morphological skills, *Applied Psycholinguistics*7, 101-127.

Gee, J. & W. Goodhart

1985 Nativization, linguistic theory & deaf language acquisition, *Sign Language Studies*49, 291-342.

Gelb, I.

1952 *A Study of Writing.*Chicago: Chicago University Press.

Greenberg, M.

1980 Social interaction between deaf preschoolers & their mothers: The effects of communication method & communication competence, *Developmental Psychology* 16, 465-474.

1983 Family stress & child competence: Effects of early intervention for families with deaf infants, *American Annals of the Deaf* 28, 407-417.

Grosjean, F.
1977 The perception of rate in spoken & sign languages, *Journal of Psycholinguistic Research* 22, 408-413.
1982 *Life with Two Languages*.Cambridge, MA: Harvard U.

Gustason, G., D. Pfetzing & E. Zawolkow
1972 *Signing Exact English*.Rossmoor, CA: Modern Signs Press.

Hancock, I.
1971 A survey of the pidgins & creoles of the world. In *Pidginization & Creolization of Languages*, Hymes ed. Cambridge: Cambridge Uuniversity Press.

Hanna, P., R. Hodges & J. Hanna
1971 *Spelling: Structure & Strategies*. Boston: Houghton-Mifflin.

Haffleld, N., F. Caccamise, & P. Siple.
1978 Deaf students' language competencies: A bilingual perspective, *American Annals of the Deaf* 123, 847-851.

Jakobson, R.
1958 Typological studies & their contributions to historical comparative linguistics. *Proceedings of the VIIIth International Congress of Linguistics*.Oslo, pp. 17-25.

Jasso, R.
1989 Why we can't understand the interpreters. *Silent News*.

Johnson, R. & C. Erting
1989 Ethnicity & socialization in a classroom for deaf children. In Lucas (ed.) 1989.

Johnson, R., S. Liddell, & C. Erting
    1989 *Unlocking the curriculum: Principles for achieving access in deaf education.* Working Paper 89-3 Gallaudet Research Institute.
Kannapell, B.
    1989 An examination of deaf college students' attitudes toward ASL & English. In Lucas (ed.) 1989.
Kay, P. & G. Sankoff
    1974 A language-universals approach to pridgins and creoles. In *Pidgins & Creoles: Current Trends and Prospects.* DeCamp & Hancock, eds. Washington, DC: Georgetown University Press.
Kidd, D.
    [1988 A comparison of comprehension of three sign language systems. Unpublished master's thesis. Universiy of Texas at Austin.]
Kluwin, T.
    1981 The grammaticality of manual representations of English in classroom settings, *American Annals of the Deaf*127, 417-421.
Krashen, S., R. Scarcella & M. Long (eds.)
    1982 *Child–adult differences in Second Language Acquisition.* Rowley, MA: Newbury House.
Kuykendall, S.
    [1990 What deaf clients want from interpreting. Unpublished master's thesis. University of Texas at Austin.]
Lane, H.
    1985 *When the Mind Hears.* New York: Random House.
Langston, C. & M. Maxwell
    1988 Holistic judgements of texts by deaf & ESL students. *Sign Language Studies*60, 295-312.

Lee, D.
  1982 Are there really signs of diglossia? Reexamining the
       situation. *Sign Language Studies*35, 127-115
  [1983 Sources and aspects of code-switching in the signing of
       a deaf adult & her interlocutors. Unpublished doctoral
       dissertation, University of Texas at Austin.]
Le Page, R. & A. Tabouret-Keller
  1985 *Acts of Identity: Creole-based approaches to language
       & Ethnicity.* London & NY: Cambridge University Press.
Ling, D.
  1976 *Speech & the Hearine-Impaired Child.* Washington: A.
G. Bell Association.
Livingston, S.
  1983 Levels of development in the language of deaf children.
       *Sign Language Studies*40, 193-286.
Lucas, C. (ed.)
  1989 *The Sociolinnguistics of the Deaf Communitv.* San
       Diego, CA: Academic Press.
- - - - -, & C. Valli
  1989 Language contact in the American Deaf Community. In
       Lucas (ed.) 1989.
Luetke-Stahlman, B.
  1983 Using bilingual instructional models in teaching
       hearing- impaired students, *American Annals of the
       Deaf*128, 873-877.
Macnamara, J.
  1967 The bilingual's linguistic performance: A psychological
       overview, *Journal of Social Issues*23, 59-77.
Marmor, G. & L. Pettito
  1979 Simultaneous communication in the classroom: How
       well is English represented? *Sign Language Studies* 23,
       99-136.

Maxvell, M.

1983a Language acquisition in a deaf child of deaf parents: Signs, sign variations, speech & print. In *Children's Language IV*, Nelson ed. Hillsdale, NJ: Erlbaum.

1983b Simultaneous communication in the classroom: What do deaf children learn? *Sign Language Studies* 39, 95-112.

1985 Sign language instruction & teacher preparation, *Sign Language Studies* 47:173-180.

1987 The acquisition of English bound morphemes in sign form, *Sign Language Studies* 57, 323-352.

1989 A signing deaf child's use of speech, *Sign Language Studies* 62, 23-42.

- - - - - ,&M. Bernstein

1985 The synergy of sign & speech in simultaneous communication, *Applied Psycholinguistics* 6, 63-81.

Maxwell, M., M. Bernstein & K. Matthews

1990 Bimodal language production. In *Theoretical issues in Sign Language Research II*, Siple ed. Chicago: U. of Chicago Press.

Maxwell, M. & P. Kraemer

i.p. Speech and identity in deaf narratives, *Text.*

Maxwell, M. & S. Smith-Todd

1986 Black sign language & school integration in Texas, *Language in Society* 15, 81-94.

Mayberry, R. & S. Tuchman

1983 Memory for sentences in ASL: The influence of age on first sign learning. In Stokoe & Volterra (eds.) 1985.

Meadow, K.

1968 Early manual communication in relation to the deaf child's intellectual, social & communicative functioning, *American Annals of the Deaf* 113, 29-41.

Meath-Lang, B., F. Caccamise & J. Albertini
    1978 Deaf persons' views on English language learning:
        Educational & sociolinguistic implications. In *Social
        Aspects of Deafness: Vol. 5, Interpresonal
        Communilcation & Deaf People.* Washington: Gallaudet
        College Department of Sociology.
Moores, D., K. Weiss & M. Goodwin
    1978 Early education programs for hearing-impaired children:
        Major findings, *American Annals of the Deaf*123, 925-
        936.
Nash, J. & A. Nash
    1981 *Deafness in Society.* NY: Lexington Books.
Newton, L.
    1985 Linguistic environment of the deaf child: A focus on
        teachers' use of nonliteral language, *Journal of Speech
        & Hearing Research*28, 336-344.
Nowell, E.
    1989 Conversational features & gender in ASL. In Lucas
        (ed.) 1989.
Paradis, M.
    1977 Bilingualism & aphasia. In *Studies in Neurolinguistics*,
        Vol. III, H. & H. A. eds. NY: Academic Press.
    1980 Language & thought in bilinguals. *The Sixth LACUS
        Forum1979.* NY: Columbia University Press.
    1981 Neurolinguistic organization of a bilingual's two
        languages. *The Seventh LACUS Forum 1980.*NY:
        Columbia University Press.
- - - - -(ed.)
    1980 *Aspects of Bilingualism.* Columbia, SC: Hornbeam.
Peters, A.
    1983 *The Units of Language Acquisition.* London: Cambridge
        University Press.

Picheny, M., N. Durlach & L. Braida
    1985 Speaking clearly for the hard of hearing I: Intelligibility
        differences between clear & conversational speech,
        *Journal of Speech & Hearing Research*28, 96103.
    1986 Speaking clearly for the hard of hearing II: Acoustic
        characeristics of clear and conversational speech,
        *Journal of Speech & Hearing Research*29, 434-446.
    1989 Speaking clearly for the hard of hearing III: An attempt
        to determine the contribution of speaking rate to
        differences in intelligibility between clear and
        conversational speech, *Journalof Speech & Hearing
        Research*32, 600-603.
Quigley, S. & C. King
    1980 Syntactic performance of hearing-impaired & normal
        hearing individuals,*Applied Psvcholinguistics* 1, 329-
        356.
Raffin, M., J. Davis & L Gilman
    1978 Comprehension of inflectional morphemes by deaf
        children exposed to a visual English sign system,
        *Journal of Speech & Hearing Research*21, 387-400.
Ramsey, C
    1989 Language planning in deaf education. InLucas ed.
        1989.
Reilly, J. & M. McIntire
    1980 American Sign Language and Pidgin Sign Language:
        What's the difference? *Sign Language Studies*27, 151-
        192.
Reilly, J., McIntire, M., & U. Bellud
    1990 Baby Face: A new perspective on universals in
        language acquisition. In Siple ed. 1978.

Sankoff, G. & S. Laberge
   1974 On the acquisition of native speakers by a language. In
        Pidgins & Creoles: Current Trends and Prospects.
        DeCamp & Hancock, eds. Washington, DC:
        Georgetown University Press.
Schlesinger, H. & K. Meadow
   1972 *Sound and Sign.*Berkeley: Univ.of CaliforniaPress.
Schmandt-Besserat, D.
   1982 The earliest precursor of writing. In *Human
        Communication.* Wang ed. San Francisco: Freeman.
Schumann, J.
   1978 *The Pidginization Process: A Model for Second
        Language Acquisition.* Rowley, MA: Newbury House.
Skutnabb-Kangas, T.
   1983 *Bilingualism or Not: The Education of Minorities.*
        Boston, MA: Little, Brown.
Slobin, D. & C. Welsh
   1973 Elicited imitation as a research tool in developmental
        psycholinguistics. In *Studies of Child Language
        Development.* Ferguson & Slobin eds. New York: Holt.
Snow, C.
   1977 Mothers' speech research: From input to interaction. In
        Talking to Children: Language Input & Acquisition,
        Ferguson & Snow eds. NY & London: Cambridge
        University Press.
Steward, W.
   1968 A sociolinguistic typology for describing national
        multilingualism. In *Readings in the Sociology of
        Language,* Fishman ed. The Hague: Mouton.
Stokoe, W.
   1970 Sign language diglossia, *Studies in Linguistics* 21, 27-
        41.

1972 A classroom experiment in two languages. In *Psycholinguistics & Total Communication: The State of the Art,*O'Rourke ed. Washington, DC: American Annals of the Deaf.

- - - - - , D. Casterline & C. Croneberg

1965 *A Dictionarv of American Sign Language on Linguistic Principles.*Washington: Gallaudet College Press [rev/. 1976, Linstok Press].

Strong, M.

1988 A bilingual approach to the education of young deaf children: ASL & English. In *Language Learning & Deafness,* Strong ed. NY: Cambridge University Press.

- - - - -& E. Charlson

1989 Simultaneous communication: How teachers approach an impossible task, *American Annals of the Deaf*134.

Stuckless, R. & J. Birch

1966 The influence of early manual communication on the linguistic development of deaf children, *American Annals of the Deaf* 106,436-480.

Supalla, S.

[1986 Manually coded English: The modality question in signed language development. Unpublished master's thesis, University of Illinois, Champaign-Urbana.]

[1990 Segmentation of manually coded English: Problems in the mapping of English in the visual-gestural mode. Unpublished doctoral dissertation, University of Illinois,Champaign-Urbana.]

Swisher, M.

1983 Characteristics of hearing mothers' manually coded English. In *SLR '83,* Stokoe & Volterra eds. Silver Spring, MD & Rome: Linstok Press, Inc. &CNR.

1984 Signed input of hearing mothers to deaf children., *Language Learning*34, 69-86.

- - - - -,& M. Thompson

  1985 Mothers learning simultaneous communicalion: The
      dimensions of the task, *American Annals of the Deaf*
      130, 212-217.

Tannen, D.

  1982 Oral & literate strategies in spoken & written narrative,
      Language in Society 58, 1-21.

Titone, R

  1983 Second language learning: An integrated psycho-
      linguistic model. In *The Sociogenesis of Language &
      Human Conduct,* Bain ed. NY: Plenum Press.

Traugott, E.

  1977 Pidginization, creolization, & language change. In
      Valdman (ed.) 1977.

Valdman, A. (ed.)

  1977 *Pidgin & Creole Linguistics.*Bloomington, IN: Indiana
      University Press.

Wampler, D.

  1971 *Linguistics of Visual English.*cSanta Rosa, CA: Early
      Childhood Educ. Dept., Santa Rosa City Schools.

Weinreich, U.

  1953 *Languages in Contact: Findings & Problems.*The
      Hague: Mouton.

Wilbur, R.

  1979 *American Sign Language & Sign Systems.* Baltimore:
      University Park Press

  1987 *American Sign Language: Linguistic & Applied
      Dimensions.* Boston, MA: Little, Brown.

Williams, J.

  1980 Bilingual experiences of a deaf child. In *Sign & Culture,*
      Stokoe ed. Silver Spring, Md.: Linstok Press.

Winston, E.
    1989 Transliteration: What's the message? In Lucas (ed.)
        1989.
Woodward, J.
    1973 Some characteristics of Pidgin Sign English, *Sign
        Language Studies*3, 39-46.
    1976 Black Southern Signing, *Language in Society* 5, 211-
        218.
- - - - - , & T. Allen
    1987 Classroom use of ASL by teachers, *Sign Language
        Studies*54, 1-10.

SIMULTANEOUS COMMUNICATION:

A DESCRIPTION BY DEAF PROFESSIONALS WORKING IN AN EDUCATIONAL SETTING

William Newell, Michael Stinson,
Diane Castle, Dominique Mallery-Ruganis,
Barbara Ray Holcomb

Abstract

Simultaneous communication (SC) was analyzed from the perspective of 36 professionals who are deaf and working in a post–secondary program for deaf students. A focus group methodology was used to generate discussion regarding features of effective SC. Comments generated during discussions were grouped into the following categories: (a) expressive sign production features, (b) body language and facial expression, (c) oral/aural and simultaneous features, (d) relationship of English and ASL, (e) communication strategies, and (f) the affective domain. In the hands of an experienced practitioner, SC involves the effective combination of aspects of both ASL and English. Deaf professionals in this study indicated that SC, when utilized by an experienced communicator and when "grounded" in effective signing can be an effective medium for communication.

Introduction

Simultaneous communication (SC) is a method of communicating through the simultaneous use of speech with signs or fingerspelling or both (Caccamise & Newell, 1984). It is currently a widely used method of communicating in educational programs for deaf students at all levels (Akamatsu, Stewart & Bonkowski, 1988). Surveys on communication methods used with deaf students indicate that sign communication is used with approximately two-thirds of the students (Jordan & Karchmer, 1986), and that this signing tends to be for the most part English-like (Allen & Woodward, 1987). This English-like signing is compatible with speaking and/or mouthing of words, and is, therefore, consistent with the evidence regarding the widespread use of SC. In addition, SC is a method of communication which, in certain contexts and between fluent users, permits adult-level, interesting conversations. Information can apparently be exchanged with ease and fluency (Maxwell & Bernstein, 1985). Thus, knowledge about production and comprehension of SC is of educational and potentially social importance.

Factors related to effective SC. Much recent research on SC has focused on the extent to which the visual/gestural channel or sign production represents English. Strong and Charlson (1987), on the basis of their own work and that of earlier investigators such as Marmor and Pettito (1979) and Kluwin (1981) have concluded that the manual component of SC does not represent English because many of the signs are omitted and those that are produced are often ungrammatical. However, these studies have generally based their conclusions of "ungrammaticality" on a comparison of the signing with the rules of written English. This comparison does not adequately consider the differences in English which occur because of modality (spoken vs. written) and which may be expected to occur when English is signed. Other authors, such as Maxwell and Bernstein (1985), have focused on the adequacy of the semantic representation of the signing in relation to speech. Maxwell and Bernstein concluded that the two channels are overwhelmingly equivalent in terms of meaning when used in the hands of skilled communicators. As Akamatsu, Stewart and Bonkowski (1988) have pointed out, however, even for this aspect of SC which has received the greatest research attention, much remains to be learned regarding factors affecting comprehension and production of SC. For example, to what extent would adult deaf SC communicators emphasize the degree of English vs. ASL grammaticality of the sign channel for ease of comprehension of SC? Preliminary studies of fluent English-based signing would indicate that fluent English signing is better conceptualized as a "contact variety" or "dialect" of ASL and includes rule governed incorporation of ASL features (Lucas & Valli, 1989).

By definition, SC requires speaking or mouthing the message as well as signing it, and some research on SC has provided information regarding the speech-hearing channel. Maxwell and Bernstein (1985) have stated that in SC, speech and sign complement each other and that people are not expected to understand SC without the speech channel. Winston (1989) discusses mouthing of English words during transliteration by interpreters. She indicates that transliterators use mouthing to reduce potential ambiguity in the manual mode. The mouthing is used to indicate which particular English word is being transliterated; e.g., the sign MUST accompanied by mouthing of "will," "should," or "have to." Akamatsu, Stewart and Bonkowski (1988) report that the SC of teachers in their research was basically speech driven, in the sense that sign production was modified to fit with a relatively unmodified speech channel. Prosodic features of speech, however, such as rate, rhythm and juncture as well as overall discourse patterns of organization may be affected in SC, but have not been adequately investigated (Whitehead, 1988).

Other factors that may be important for effective communication with SC are facial expression, body language, special communication strategies, and expression of affect. In regard to body language and facial expression, Kluwin and Kluwin (1983) noted the importance of incorporating these features into

SC for effective instruction. For example, certain head and body movements as well as facial expressions are desirable when the teacher is asking a question. The significance of body language and facial expression in carrying linguistic information in American Sign Language (ASL) has also been described (e.g., Baker & Padden, 1978).

Several writers, Roth and Spekman (1984), Foster, Barefoot and DeCaro (1989), and Kluwin and Kluwin (1983), have recognized that successful communication involves more than just competent production of the signal. It also involves selective use of special strategies to increase the effectiveness of communication for particular situations or audiences. For example, Kluwin and Kluwin (1983) suggest that in an extended discussion of a topic, the transitions from one subtopic to another must be clearly indicated by pauses. In addition, Akamatsu, Stewart, and Bonkowski (1988) have postulated that speech and sign will be primarily English-like in effective SC, but in certain situations, such as in repeating an explanation, experienced users of SC shift to an ASL-like presentation. Davis (1989) discusses code-switching and mixing as a phenomenon of fluent contact-variety English-like signing.

Effective communication also involves transmission of appropriate affect (Woolfolk & Brooks, 1983; Robinson, 1972). Such cues as distance, posture, facial expression, and hesitation contribute to the aesthetics and comfort of the communication (Woolfolk & Brooks, 1983). The affective tone accompanying the speech and sign would be expected to influence the audience's reaction to the communication.

Purpose

Previous research on SC has generally collected and analyzed samples of SC from the perspective of the researcher, often drawing conclusions regarding the desirability of certain features (e.g., Strong and Charlson, 1987; Marmor & Petitto, 1979; Kluwin & Kluwin, 1983). What would the conclusions be if, instead, deaf persons themselves were asked what is desirable in SC? Perspectives of deaf people may contribute to an expanded view of what is involved in successful communication with SC. In this research deaf people were asked for their opinions regarding features of SC they saw as important and for insights regarding the relative contribution of different features to the overall effectiveness of SC as a communication mode.

Method. In this study, focus group interviews were used, in which small groups of deaf faculty and staff working in a post secondary educational setting discussed their views of SC. A major benefit of focus group meetings is that members stimulate each other in generating ideas (Calder, 1977). The interviews were open-ended, and participants were encouraged to pursue their own line of reasoning. It was the responsibility of the moderator to ensure that certain major issues were addressed; however, there was no particular order in which topics had to be covered (Bogdan and Biklen, 1982; Calder, 1977). In addition, at the end of the focus group interviews, participants were asked to rank categories that described SC, in order to obtain further information on the relative importance of different categories.

Characteristics of Participants.[1] Deaf and hard–of–hearing faculty and staff (hereafter we will use the term 'deaf' to refer to all participants) working in a post secondary educational setting were contacted to participate in focus groups. Each person was asked to

---

[1] It should be noted that participants in this study were primarily college-educated and professional employees of a post-secondary program for deaf students with primarily oral and mainstream educational backgrounds. As a group, however, the participants preferred that signing with or without speech rather than speech alone be used in communicating with them. Deaf persons (adults and students) with different communicational, educational, occupational, and social backgrounds might provide different perspectives on SC from those of these participants.

fill out a 10-item questionnaire about their hearing loss, communication preference, and educational background. A total of 36 persons participated in the focus group sessions.

Responses to the questionnaire indicated that twenty-six participants lost their hearing by age 2, seven between ages 2–12 years, and three at age 16 or older. Ten described their unaided hearing level as moderate to severe (40–95dB) while 26 reported a profound hearing level (95dB or greater). Sign language was learned by eight participants before age five, by five between 6–15 years, and by 23 at the age of 16 or older. All participants used sign language with or without speech at the time of this study. Participants included persons with backgrounds in residential, day classes and mainstream public school settings. There were 22 women and 14 men in the participant group.

Procedure. Six focus groups, with five or six deaf professionals in each, participated in group discussions lasting approximately two hours. Participants were sorted into the six focus groups based on degree of their preference for and background in sign language. Groups ranged from strong preference and primary background in sign language to moderate preference and limited educational experience with sign language. Participants were asked to think about persons who express themselves very well using sign and speech together and to "picture" these persons communicating. With this context, participants were asked to react to the following questions:

1. What is the person doing that makes his or her communication clear and easy to understand?

2. What is the person doing to make his or her communication enjoyable to watch, "read", and perhaps, hear.

After this initial group discussion, participants watched three videotapes, each three minutes in length, of experienced signers using SC. The first signer was deaf and had been signing for approximately 55 years. The second signer was a hearing child of deaf parents who had been signing for approximately 50 years, and the third signer was a hearing professional who had been signing for approximately 20 years. After each videotape, participants were asked to discuss further ideas regarding the strengths and weaknesses of each signer, as related to the two questions discussed in the initial part of the session.

The moderator of the focus groups was a deaf professional. The note taker, who wrote participants' comments on newsprint throughout the meetings, was hearing and was assisted in taking extensive notes by a voice interpreter. The same moderator, note taker and interpreter were used in all six focus groups.

The discussion was recorded on both audio-and videotape. Verbatim typed transcripts were generated from the audio tapes and reviewed for accuracy by the focus group moderator and note taker utilizing the videotapes.

The typed transcripts were reviewed to generate 41 categories in which similar comments were grouped. Subsequently two coders, working independently, coded each of the over 400 comments (phrase, sentence or paragraph) contained in the typed transcripts into one of these categories. Differences in coding between coders were resolved through discussion. (A comparison paper reports how the 41 categories were ranked in order of relative importance by the focus group participants (Stinson, Newell, Castle, Mallery-Ruganis, & Ray-Holcomb, 1990). The 41 categories were then collapsed into 16 larger categories in writing the following summary of the discussions.

Results

Participants made extensive and varied comments on the features of SC they saw as important and offered numerous insights on how different features contributed to the overall effectiveness of the message when SC is employed. Participants' comments are grouped into the following general dimensions: expressive sign production features; body language/facial expression; oral/aural and simultaneous features; the relationship of English and ASL; communication strategies; and the affective domain.

Expressive Sign Production Features. Participants in the focus groups mentioned many features of expressive sign production which are important to them in the context of SC. Four basic categories will be described: (a) clarity of production, (b) prosody (pace, pausing, smoothness), (c) sign choice/semantics, and (d) grammatical features.

Clarity of production. Participants commented on the importance of clear production of individual signs and fingerspelling, the position of the hands and use of the appropriate signing space, and the overall intelligibility of the expressive sign signal (all factors taken together). Most of the following comments were based on experiences with simultaneous communicators who were not effective communicators of SC:

...the sign production on EXPERIENCE...and on FEELING...and on WORLD were inappropriate....It seemed like he didn't finish his sign production, but his hand was still there like he should get rid of that one hand. He seemed to be signing with one hand...

I hate to see people sign like, "elbow sign language," I call it. They keep their elbows in or they put their elbows on the table or sign in a very limited space and...they should be natural and moving their elbows and. having a normal space...

I think fingerspelling also should be very clear and it should be very slow. They shouldn't just whiz it through the air.

Prosody (pace, pausing, smoothness). Features of the expressive sign channel related to the rhythm, pace, pausing structure, and smoothness of signing were important to our focus group participants. Their comments supported signing that was not hurried but well paced with appropriate pausing (presumably at phrase and sentence boundaries) and characterized as "smooth:"

I think a slower pace is important, too, especially with simcom. If you're not using voice and you're signing fast, ya know, that works fine. But if you're trying to talk at the same time you are signing, you almost need to slow down.

...he was going too fast. He wasn't thinking about his pacing. He wasn't really pacing the information. You know, just going, going, going as if everyone was understanding his talk...

The need to maintain appropriate pace is important to comfort as well as comprehension. The following quotation is illustrative.

We need breaks periodically. Sometimes when they are signing continuously in one sentence and then the other sentence comes, and I need time to figure out what's being said, so we need some pauses. I'd like a visual break.

Sign Choice & Semantics. Simultaneous communication presents a unique challenge to the user, that of speaking or mouthing English while at the same time choosing signs which will communicate the meaning of the message. The focus group participants referred to the challenge to communicate meaning through signs as "signing conceptually." The following comments illustrate the importance they attach to this very complex aspect of SC:

It's really important that they sign correctly conceptually. It's important to use signs that are semantically equivalent and conceptually correct.

It's like signing, "Your nose is running," but using the sign TO-RUN as in 'jogging.' You need a different sign for 'Your nose is running.' There is a sign for 'run' and 'your nose is running' is entirely different from the sign that means 'run'. So you need to use the appropriate, semantic sign for the context.

Grammatical Features. Finally, the focus groups com-mented on the need to observe the grammatical principles of ASL. The grammatical feature mentioned most often was the use of effective space (the three dimensionality of signing space) to establish referents. Participants mentioned the need to use a specific directionality of movement for verb signs to show subjects and objects:

The ASL principles like directionality--someone says, "Please give me the ball." But the principles have to be correct. If I sign it like GIVE HIM instead of GIVE-ME, that will be confusing.

Another grammatical aspect mentioned included use of the QUOTATION-MARKS sign to indicate that you are expressing something more literally in English signs or fingerspelling. This is similar to Davis (1989) who discusses the use by interpreters of the QUOTATION-MARKS sign to "flag" or "mark" fingerspelled words or metaphoric phrases:

For example, the phrase, 'cream of the crop,' may be confusing....Clarify what it means... Yes, using quotation marks (for that) is important ...

Participants also commented on use of a head nod to express "state of being:"

For example, with *is* and *am*: 'My name is [participant's sign name].' I think I'd use some other techniques, maybe even a head nod. MY NAME and a head nod for 'is' [then the sign name].

Modifying sign movement by changing the force of movement, the length of movement and/or the time of movement within a sign can modify the meaning. Participants felt this aspect of sign grammar was important in SC.

I like it when they can express their emotions and tone variation through their sign, instead of their voice. Show they are angry,... the movement of their hands, instead of just saying "angry"... putting the emphasis on the sign.

Finally, participants mentioned the need to use classifiers (handshapes that represent specific classes of objects) and signs that incorporate number and time elements into the sign. The following two comments illustrate:

Classifiers like showing the car with the 3-finger handshape for the car, as opposed to signing straight English, 'My car hit something.' A person would use ASL and then classifiers to say that they got into an accident.

A person should use ASL features like TWO–DAYS–AGO or THREE–DAYS–AGO in one sign as opposed to signing TWO DAY+S in straight English.

Body Language and Facial Expression. Participants addressed the importance of signers' using what they called "body language" and "facial expression" for two purposes: to express feelings and as grammatical structures. First, these characteristics seemed to be related to being "animated, dramatic and expressive." As one participant put it:

It [facial expression and body language] is what deaf culture is. It's what makes it (signing) an attraction to deaf culture and the people in deaf culture.

And as another participant commented:

So with the deaf person, it's the body language and the facial expression and you get more of a feeling ... if communicators are not really using a lot of facial expression or body language, you lose a lot of the tone of the communication.

Secondly, what participants called "body language" clearly relates to the use of certain body postures, body movements (shifts) and facial expressions to serve grammatical purposes:

I would suggest one more thing...that is the use of spacing. If you're talking about 2 or 3 people and you are talking and explaining, ya know, you would shift your body to clarify, instead of just standing straight. And I told him...The body movement shows...who is speaking.

This use of body shift to indicate "role" in narrative is documented in the research literature (Padden, 1986). What was referred to as "body language, mime, and pantomime" as in the following is described in the research literature as use of the body as a classifier (Supalla, 1986):

So he showed that he was assuming the character of the dummy...

He kind of acted out the important points within the story... He really didn't sign them in English. He almost pantomimed some of it.

Participants also indicated that "facial expression" carried grammatical function.

Use facial expression and movement of sign to represent what you are saying. Yeah, to represent articles and the verb, *to be.*

Oral/aural and simultaneous features of SC were also important to the focus group participants. These comments were concerned with (a) clear lip movement, (b) use of voice, (c) simultaneous production features, (d) matching intonation, and (e) the use of fingerspelling and speech.

Lip movement. By definition, SC involves mouthing or voicing English while signing. The participants described desirable lip movement with adjectives like *clear* and *natural.*

His mouth movement is so clear. You know if he didn't move his hands, I would still understand.

Participants expressed frustration in trying to lip read speakers and signers who produced lip movement of poor quality. Reasons for difficulty in lip reading included lack of appropriate lip movements, exaggerated lip movement and a mustache that interferes with visibility of lip movements.

I know some folks can't help this, but...they have stiff lips and they don't enunciate well when they are signing, it's just not a natural lip movement.

Sometimes they have really...exaggerated lip movements. They should use normal lip movement. Exaggerating makes me feel stupid.

They need clear mouth movement that's easy to speech read with no real distracting features. Distractions might be a mustache that hangs over your lip.

Use of voice. Most comments about the use of voice with SC are from participants who wear hearing aids and gain some benefit from sound cues. For them, the addition of voice makes the SC easier to understand, e.g., when a sign is not clearly produced or is unfamiliar, when a fingerspelled or lip read word is missed. For some participants, the process of matching sound with lip movement gives a degree of reinforcement to the overall communication. One participant indicates the sound of a voice was especially helpful in locating the speaker in a group setting. The following comments were prompted after watching the videotapes with and without sound:

....the voice helped too. If I missed the fingerspelling, between the voice and the mouth movement, that helped a lot.

. . . I can depend on my hearing aids . . . But without (sound) . . . it required intense concentration. . . to figure out what he was talking about . . . because of the way he was signing.

I don't understand speech with hearing alone, but when I can hear the sound and match it with the lip movement and then have reinforcement of sign, all three together work the best for me.

It appears from participant comments that use of clear English lip movements or voice or both with signing were most critical when the respondent had to understand an inarticulate, ineffective signer. A few participants mentioned specific disadvantages to hearing the sounds of a voice; an irritating voice quality or accent may interfere with understanding:

It was hard to concentrate...because his voice was...very irritating ...it sounded like ...static.

If I'm with a person whose voice is not very clear or if they have an accent ...I get a mixed signal. It's like what I'm hearing doesn't match with what I'm seeing.

The discussion of lip movement and voice suggests that participants put primary emphasis on clear signing and utilize lip movement and/or voice to help clarify ambiguities. A participant philosophically summed up the issue on the use of voice with the comment, "...It just depends on how a person receives communication comfortably."

Simultaneous production features. The focus group participants commented on the importance of the simultaneity of the signal in SC. These comments in general refer to congruence in timing and meaning between the spoken signal and the signed signal.

When the signer presents two different messages in the signed and spoken channels, the deaf person has to work at trying to figure out the meaning to avoid misunderstandings. One participant expressed it this way:

I really depend on watching both the lip movement and the signs and sometimes if there's not congruence between the two, if the signs don't match the lip movement, I really get confused and then communication breaks down.

Another observation related to the timing of lip movements accompanying signs. It is important for the message on the lips to occur at the same time as the signs, not before or after the sign:

[He] tended to speak faster than he signed... It's like he'd say the word, "boy," and then the sign for BOY would happen after it. But I'd rather it'd happen at the same time.

Matching intonation. Another part of simultaneity is showing on the hands, face, and/or body the expression typically conveyed by the voice. The meaning of the message, including the prosody (pauses, rate, intonation) should be communicated visually.

. . . they should put it into their face, their expression . . . voice intonation shows where they have a pause . . . You can hear it, but they are not showing it in the signed language . . .

. . .he incorporates what hearing people do with their voice, the inflection, he incorporates that in his hands, especially in fingerspelling.

Use of fingerspelling and speech. Some participants noted the importance of simultaneously using English lip movement with fingerspelling. For those people, the location of the hand when fingerspelling is important.

. . . people articulate a word on their lips, sometimes it just can't be lip read . . . and I'll rely on the fingerspelling to try and understand it. But they need to do it at the same time."

. . . it was important about the position of the fingerspelling. Don't finger-spell over your lips.

Relationship of English and ASL. Participants discussed the relationship between English and ASL. There was general consensus that for SC the basic structure of signing follows English word order and that "clear lip movement" is important. Some participants described "good" SC signers as people who "have good ASL or knowledge of the ASL principles in signed English . . . like space, (and) directionality."

Participants also referred to certain teachers they felt were very clear who could combine ASL with clear mouth movement:

. . . when I was at (college) I noticed that many of us tended to prefer teachers who could sign ASL, but also had really clear mouth movements. There was one teacher . . . who kind of signed okay—it wasn't really ASL, but he had really clear mouth movements and I know students tended to take a lot of courses from him. I have clear recollections of which teachers we thought were really good and clear. Mouth movement was definitely a factor in deciding that.

Communication Strategies. In SC, sign, speech production and non-manual features carry most of the responsibility for transmission of the message. However, the focus group discussions indicated that these domains are not sufficient for effective communication. In addition, there are particular strategies that are primarily related to adaptation to the communication situation or audience which can increase the effectiveness of the communication. The most frequently discussed of these strategies was the use of fingerspelling to support sign. Two other sets of strategies which participants discussed pertained to adaptation of signing in response to setting, and to effective organization of information.

Fingerspelling as a support strategy. Participants describe five ways in which fingerspelling was used as a support strategy: to give a sign a specific meaning, to give emphasis to a particular word, to introduce new vocabulary, to indicate inflectional endings, and to mark English idioms. A sign can often be translated using several different but relatively synonymous English words. In SC, fingerspelling helps clarify which particular English word the signer intends. Two comments participants made regarding this strategy were:

I'd rather have the sign along with the fingerspelled word because sometimes lip reading does not help. For example, when she first said *infant*, I thought she was saying *invest* along with the sign BABY; oh no; after (I saw the) fingerspelling (of) the word, I understood it.

I prefer that if someone is using a word that doesn't really have a separate sign, that they fingerspell it and then use a close synonym and then use that sign throughout the lecture or whatever.

Note here that the participant specified that the word should be fingerspelled before the sign is produced. This point was also mentioned by others.

When a sign is not used in a familiar way, it is important to add fingerspelling. One participant gave the example of a person saying, *poetic license,* and using the sign FREEDOM, for *license.* The word, *license,* might have been more understandable if it had also been fingerspelled.

Sometimes an effective way to give emphasis to a particular word is to fingerspell it, even though there is a sign which conveys the specific word in a clear manner. Comments pertinent to this point were:

Yeah; I think when he fingerspelled at the end, he really emphasized what he was saying like, *ball*. He'd fingerspell b-a-l-l and then pause at the end of that.

One strategy mentioned by a participant indicated that it is important to signal that a word will be fingerspelled.

Well, if you have a person who is signing and then all of a sudden fingerspells, it might help if they use the non-dominant hand to point--literally point at the hand they are fingerspelling with for additional emphasis.

A related way of using fingerspelling to support sign is to introduce new vocabulary with fingerspelling. If others are not likely to know either the word or the sign, the word can be fingerspelled and then followed by a sign.

In addition to giving a specific meaning to a sign, people sometimes support English language usage by fingerspelling words where an inflectional ending is important or by fingerspelling all words in an English idiom:

I would fingerspell those, I wouldn't (sign) running. I don't do RUN and then ING, I would do running, R-U-N-N-I-N-G for *running* because I am a fingerspeller.

Another person commented:

For example, I noticed that   he didn't always use the sign, he would fingerspell, like M-U-R-D-E-R. He would fingerspell it, things like that, H-E G-O-T A-W-A-Y W-I-T-H M-U-R-D-E-R. He didn't sign that because it's an idiom. So it's important to emphasize the English idiom.

Setting. Most of the discussion regarding adaptation to setting pertained to primarily ASL or "English" signing. Participants suggested that specific situations and the communication needs/preferences of the audience determine when ASL and sign English are more appropriate. Participants thought sign English was more appropriate when the classroom was the main setting. Some examples:

For educational purposes or educational settings, I think pretty much exact English word order is what's called for, very limited use of ASL.

I like ASL, myself, but in a specific situation, I want English or technical vocabulary...

In contrast, ASL tends to be used in informal situations or in meetings intended primarily for deaf persons, such as a National Association of the Deaf meeting. As one woman said:

ASL tends to be more of a social and an informal situation when it's used. Say for example family, or if there was a...deaf conference....

Participants felt that it was important to closely adhere to English in some classes more than in others. For example, in an English class it is important to include articles in the signing, but in an electronics class it might not be required.

Another way that signers vary in use of ASL and English is code switching from sign English to ASL, and vice versa. Some participants suggested that the extent of code switching depends on the communication needs of the particular audience. One woman explained that if she is using English and she sees that an idea "goes right over his head and misses the point," she quickly changes to ASL.

The amount of space used in signing is also influenced by the setting. In the classroom, it is desirable to use more space in signing than in one-to-one communication.

Organization and conciseness. Correct sign selection and emphasis, along with an orderly presentation of ideas, is important for effective communication. One participant indicated that signing needs to emphasize the critical words in the sentence and not give equal emphasis to all words. Another participant said:

They (signers) need a more organized presentation, using a sign to indicate a flow of organized information, a more structured flow of ideas. When people skip from point to point, it's really hard to follow.

Another discussed conciseness:

Yes, if it goes on too long, it can get confusing. So they need to be shorter phrases so that it's clear and to the point.

Insertion of visual breaks between ideas during a period of uninterrupted signing also helps achieve an orderly, easily understood presentation. This use of visual breaks, as well as breaks from continuous signing by insertion of a different activity, were included in the following comment:

Sometimes when I'm looking and they are signing and signing, ya know, my eyes get tired. We need breaks periodically. Sometimes when they are signing continuously, in one sentence and then another sentence comes and I need to figure out what's being said so we need some pauses. I'd like visual break.

Affective Domain. In addition to expressive features and communication strategies the focus group participants discussed affective factors including sensitivity, comfort, openness, and acceptance which contributed to effective SC. These factors can be divided into two major areas: sensitivity and comfort and confidence in one's ability to communicate.

Sensitivity. Participants indicated that three kinds of sensitivity were important: to deafness and Deaf culture; to communication preferences; and respect for the intelligence of deaf individuals. Participants felt that being respectful and approachable were important indicators of sensitivity to deafness and Deaf culture. Respect for the deaf individual's communication preference and the use of sign language at all times within an environment where deaf students or professionals work are also important indicators of sensitivity. As one participant said:

Don't start signing just because a deaf person appears...like doing me a favor.... Everyone should sign all the time here...fact of life here. Should be a natural part of life here.

In a similar way, talking without signing in a student's presence when discussing that student was seen as "using your hearing to manipulate certain situations."

Participants provided several examples of how an individual shows sensitivity to the communication preferences of deaf persons: making an effort to communicate, ability to sign fluently in the classroom, and ability to clarify vocabulary and idioms through fingerspelling, defining and paraphrasing. In relation to effort, one participant said, "people need to make a sincere effort to communicate." It's part "of an attitude". In discussing sign fluency, it was recommended that teachers not ask students to teach them new signs in the classroom. This was construed as "taking advantage of the students knowledge" and was considered inappropriate. Teachers should have solid sign skills and therefore should not need to ask students for help in the communication process.

Respect for the intelligence of deaf persons was considered very important. Participants explained their feelings regarding this issue in the following way:

I think students should have an educational opportunity to understand whatever needs to be said. For example if someone is using a technical word, I want to see that technical word. I don't want to see it watered down....

...we're all in a highly educated level and it can be very frustrating. I went to Boston and the interpreter wasn't used to scientific language and he really brought the whole presentation down in register and that was frustrating to me.

Comfort and Confidence. Other affective factors that participants felt were important to the communication process were comfort and confidence. Communicators who are friendly, act naturally and pleasantly, use appropriate body language, and are dramatic when necessary indicate a comfort level and confidence in their ability:

When a person appears stiff, constrained and hesitant, he gives the impression of finding it difficult to adapt to Deaf culture . . .

This lack of comfort and confidence can influence all participants in a conversation:

If a person is not comfortable with sign language or simultaneous communication themselves and I know they are not comfortable, I become uncomfortable myself.

In addition, maintaining eye contact is important in indicating a person's confidence and comfort level. One participant put it this way:

...talking about eye contact...I noticed that it's related to culture. It seems that in the hearing culture... they look around and talk and, boy, that makes me sick. You have to look at me. I have to be comfortable....

Overall it was agreed that :

...a good communicator is someone who . . . considers everything and is sensitive to the needs of people that they are communicating with.

Discussion

Participants in our focus group discussions provided a rich corpus of descriptive data regarding features of SC. This data indicates that they are describing a complex bimodal act which involves the effective combination of aspects of both ASL and English. The sign component of SC described is fluent English-like signing. By this is meant signs drawn primarily from ASL, produced accurately and communicated in English word order utilizing the grammatical–inflectional devices of ASL. The oral/aural component involves clear and natural English lip movement which accompanies and is simultaneous with the sign signal. It appears that participants prefer that the pace of simultaneous communication be slower than signing ASL or speaking English.

This data would indicate that *effective* SC is primarily sign driven; i.e. an effective SC communicator must have thorough knowledge of, and automatic recall for, the "appropriate" sign(s), as well as have command of grammatical/inflectional devices of ASL. Akamatsu et. al (1988) report that the SC of teachers in their study was basically speech driven. This factor may account for other reports in the literature of ineffective SC (Kluwin, 1981, Marmor & Petitto, 1979).

Participants discussing the relationship between English and ASL and their perception that certain "good communicators" can combine these two languages are describing what has been traditionally called Pidgin Sign English (PSE) with lip movement for English (more recently described by Lucas & Valli [1989] as a contact-variety or possibly a dialect of ASL). Participants describe the best SC communicators as being thoroughly familiar with ASL vocabulary and its grammatical/inflectional features, who combine these signs and features fluently with English word order and lip movements. Sometimes they refer to this ability as "signing ASL with clear lip movements." In a letter to the Editor, published in *Silent News* (1989), a deaf man supports this same perception,

...I have always demanded ASL interpreter... with the understanding that they always mouth while signing...

This apparently contradictory notion that ASL can be combined with English lip movements is consistent with the overall description of fluent SC described by our participants. Davis (1989) describes the pheno-menon of code–mixing (the use of English mouthing during ASL communication). Apparently when the language structure is more English–like, as in SC, but the signs are conceptually accurate and ASL inflec-tional rules including nonmanual (facial expression) inflections are utilized, deaf people will describe this fluent SC as "using ASL with clear lip movement."

In addition the participants talked about the importance of communication techniques which enhance effectiveness. In this area, the use of fingerspelling to reinforce and specify English words while signing, ability to adapt signing in response to setting and audience (this includes ability to use both ASL and SC as appropriate as well as to use SC and code–switch to ASL as the discourse requires), and effectiveness of organization of information—were all considered important.

Aside from the specific productive characteristics of the signal and the importance of utilizing effective communication techniques the participants discussed the importance of appropriate attitudes of respect for deaf persons, their communicative preferences, and their Culture. Trotter (1989) discusses teacher attitudes toward ASL and signed English. In her study teachers of the deaf in training rated ASL as "more expressive, more exciting, and faster than signed English but signed English as having greater precision, more complete sentences, more consistently correct sign usages, grammar that is better, signs that are more functional, and having the ability to communicate more complete messages" (p. 225). The responses of these teachers in training showed a slightly higher positive attitude toward signed English and attributed more positive attributes to signed English but when questioned overtly regarding ASL and signed English did not show any preference. It would appear from this study that the importance attributed to attitude, as perceived by deaf professionals, has some basis in fact and that the perspectives of deaf people toward communication (languages and modalities) is an important consideration.

REFERENCES

Akamatsu, C. , D. Stewart, & N. Bonkowski
[1988 Constraining factors in the production of simultaneous communication by teachers. Paper presented at the convention of the American Educational Research Association, New Orleans, April.]

Allen, T. & J. Woodward
1987 Teacher characteristics and the degree to which teachers incorporate features of English in their sign communication with hearing-impaired students, *American Annals of the Deaf* 61-67.

Bogdan, R. & S. Biklen
1982 *Qualitative research for education.* Boston: Allyn and Bacon, Inc.

Caccamise, F. & W. Newell
1984 A review of current terminology used in deaf education & signing, *Journal of the Academy of Rehabilitative Audiology* 17, 106-129.

Calder, B.
1977 Focus groups and the nature of qualitative marketing research, *Journal of Marketing Research* 14, 353-364.

Davis, J.
1989 Distinguishing language contact phenomena in ASL interpretation. In *Sociolinguistics of the Deaf Community,,* Lucas ed. San Diego, CA: Academic Press, Inc., 85-102.

Foster, S., S. Barefoot & P. DeCaro
1989 The meaning of communication to deaf college students: A multidimensional definition, *Journal of Speech & Hearing Disorders* 54: 558-569.

Jordan, I. K. & M. Karchmer
  1986 Patterns of sign use among hearing-impaired students. In *Deaf Children in America,* Schildroth & Karchmer eds. San Diego: College-Hill Press.
Kluwin, T.
  1981 The grammaticality of manual representations of English in classroom settings, *American Annals of the Deaf* 126, 417-421.
- - - - -, & B. Kluwin
  1983 Microteaching as a tool for improving simultaneous communication in classrooms for hearing-impaired students, *American Annals of the Deaf* 128, 820-825.
Lucas, C. (ed.)
  1989 *The Sociolinguistics of the Deaf Community.* San Diego: Academic Press.
- - - - - & C. Valli
  1989 Language contact in the American Deaf Community. In *Sociolinguistics of the Deaf Community,* above.
Marmor, G. & L. Petitto
  1979 Simultaneous communication in the classroom: How well is English grammar represented? *Sign Language Studies* 23, 99-136.
Maxwell, M. & M. Bernstein
  1985 The synergy of sign and speech in simultaneous communication. *Applied Psycholinguistics* 6, 63-82.
Padden, C.
  1986 Verbs and Role-Shifting in ASL. In *Proceedings of the Fourth NSSLRT,* Padden ed. Silver Spring, MD: Nat'l Ass'n of the Deaf. 44-57.
Robinson, W.
  1972 *Language & Social Behavior.* London: Penguin .

Roth, F., & N. Spekman

    1984 Assessing the programmatic abilities of children: Part 1. Organizational framework & assessment parameters, *Journal ofSpeech & Hearing Disorders* 49, 2-11.

Stinson, M., Newell, Castle, Mallery-Ruganis & B. Holcomb

    [1989 Generation & ranking of descriptions of simultaneous communication by deaf professionals working in post-secondary education. Unpublished manuscript, NTID, Rochester, NY.]

Strong, M. & E. Charlson

    (i.p.) Simultaneous communication: Are teachers attempting an impossible task? *American Annals of the Deaf* 132, 376-382.

Supalla, T.

    1986 The classifier system in American Sign Language. In *Proceedings of the Fourth NSSLRT*, Padden ed. Silver Spring, MD: Nat'l Ass'n of the Deaf. 3-30.

Trotter, J.

    1989 Language attitudes of teachers of the deaf. In *Sociolinguistics of the Deaf Community*. Lucas ed. San Diego: Academic Press. 147-164.

Whitehead, R. & B. Whitehead

    [1988 Vowel duration characteristics during simultaneous communication. Paper presented at the Joint Meeting of the Acoustical Society of America & the Japan Acoustical Society, Nov. 1988, Honolulu, Hawaii.]

Winston, E.

    1989 Transliteration: What's the message? In *Sociolinguistics of Deaf Community*. Lucas ed. San Diego: Academic.

Woolfook, & Brooks

    1983 Nonverbal communication in teaching. In *Review of Research in Education.*.

    1989 Letter to the Editor, *Silent News*, Vol. 21(4), 3.

4. THE EFFECTIVENESS OF THREE MEANS OF COMMUNICATION IN THE COLLEGE CLASSROOM

Dennis R. Cokely

Abstract

The assumption in education of deaf students, for the past fifteen years at least, has been that simultaneous communication (SC) is the most effective means of communication in the classroom. Some justification for this assumption comes from research studies conducted during the past ten years, but methodological limitations of these studies, here reviewed, casts serious doubt on the conclusions claimed. Descriptive research over the past five years has lead some linguists and educators to question the effectiveness of SC and to ask whether, given the psycholinguistic demands of signing and speaking at the same time, more effective communication may occur if (hearing) people sign without speaking or speak and use an interpreter. A pilot study designed to investigate this question resulted in no unequivocal evidence of superiority, but because actual college lectures (not the usual contrived and rehearsed material) were used and notes taken by the students as well as their objective test results were examined, it appears that signing without speech does have notable advantages.

Review of research

The research studies over the past decade on classroom communication (e.g. Klopping, 1972; White and Stevenson, 1975; Newell, 1978; Caccamise and Blaisdell, 1977; Jacobs, 1977) have consistently concluded that deaf students receive information better with SC than with other means of communication. Critically reviewing these studies, however, one is forced to question and challenge these studies and their conclusions because of their methodological limitations. These limitations severely restrict the generality of results—more importantly, make suspect the validity claimed for these studies. Below are reviews of five studies representative of the research in this area.

1. *Klopping (1972)* examined the effectiveness of communication under three conditions: "Total Communication" (i.e. SC, signing and speaking at the same time), the Rochester Method (i.e. speaking and simultaneously fingerspelling the words), and speech reading with voice. The results yielded the following "effectiveness ranking" (for the 30 high School students in the study) for comprehension under these conditions: "Total Communication" (76.35%), the Rochester Method (55.10%) and speech reading with voice (35.15%).

There are several limitations on the validity of this study: (1) The stimulus materials consisted of "...four different nonfictional stories ...adapted to meet the needs of the study." Adaptation included, "...deleting idiomatic language, changing vocabulary, and shortening some of the sentences." The stimulus material, then, is based on written, not conversational, English. Given that there is ample evidence to show that written discourse and conversational discourse are quite different (Freedle, 1979, Chafe, 1980), results of the study may apply only to written material presented under the three conditions. (2) "The stories were all narrated by the investigator who was skilled in the methods of communication." No other descriptive information is given about presentation of the stimulus material. Since each of the stories was presented to six groups of students, it is reasonable to assume that the "narrator" had memorized the stories. This, of course, results in memorization behaviors which are quite different from behaviors found in conversational discourse (Freedle, 1979; Chafe, 1980). Additionally, since no discussion of the actual presentations is provided, the extent to which the narrator was able to replicate exactly each story under each condition is not known. It is conceivable that variations in the actual presentations could account for some of the reported differences in effectiveness. (3) "The stories were all narrated by the investigator..."" Apart from raising the question of whether investigator bias was a factor in this study, the obtained results may reflect the student's ability to understand the investigator under the three conditions but may not, in fact, reflect a general level of comprehension under the three conditions. To generalize, as the author does, that "...teachers should use total communication in order to achieve the highest level of comprehension of information..." based on the students" ability to understand a single individual may be attributing greater significance to the study than is warranted—especially when that single individual is the investigator.

2. *White and Stevenson (1975)* examined the effectiveness of communication under four conditions: "Total Communication" (i.e. SC again), Manual Communication, Oral Communication, and Reading. This study yielded the following "effectiveness ranking" (for the 45 high school students in the study) for comprehension: Reading, Manual Communi-cation, Total Communication, and Oral Communication. Among the findings of this study were that "...the addition of speech to manual communication did not significantly increase students" ability to assimilate information. To the contrary it seemed slightly, though not significantly, to depress it."

The limitations on the study are these: (1) The stimulus material consisted of "...16 factual passages ... taken from *Getting the Facts: Specific Skill Series* , *Book B* & *Book D*...." The stimulus material, then, was representative of written discourse and, one might add, a skewed representation at best since the passages from Book B "...were at the second grade level and passages from Book D were at the fourth grade level." As is true of the Klopping study, results of this study may only apply to written discourse presented under the four conditions. (2) The stimulus material was presented "...by an interpreter employed to present the material under all methods of communication." The only descriptive information given about the presentation of the stimulus material is that each presentation was timed by a monitor and rate of presentation was not a confounding variable. It is reasonable to assume that the interpreter memorized the various passages since the material was presented to nine groups of students. The absence of descriptive information raises the possibility that variance in the actual presentations could account for some of the reported differences in effectiveness. (3) Since the passages were all presented by the same interpreter, it is possible that the results reflect the extent to which the subjects were able to comprehend one individual's speech, manual communication and "total communication." That is, the results, while they may be an accurate indication of how well the students understood the interpreter, may not be generalizable to the four communication conditions investigated by this study. 3. *Newell (1978)* examined the extent to which deaf students (N = 28) were able to comprehend factual information under four conditions: Oral Communication, Manual Communication, Simultaneous Communication, and Interpreted Communication. The results of this study were that

"...scores on the simultaneous presentation were significantly higher than scores for the manual presentation and oral presentation [and] scores for the interpreted presentation were significantly higher than the oral presentation ."

Limitations: (1) As with the previous two studies, the stimulus material was based on written discourse: "...four factual stories adapted from *Getting the Facts, the Specific Skill Series*...." As in the Klopping study, the passages were adapted ("...deleting idiomatic language, rearranging and simplifying the structure of some paragraphs, and controlling the vocabulary"). Thus, the results of the study may only be applicable to written material presented under the four conditions. (2) No descriptive information is given concerning the actual presentation of the stimulus passages. Presumably this involved memorization (in which case the limitations discussed above would obtain), or the use of videotape (in which case the limitations discussed under the next study would obtain). In either case, presentation of the stimulus material is artificially constrained. (3) No information is given as to whether the stimulus material was presented by one or more individuals. If there was only one presenter, then the generality of the results can be questioned. If, on the other hand, more than one presenter was used, the results might be more indicative of the actual communication condition than of the performance of a single individual.

4. *Caccamise and Blaisdell (1977)* examined the accuracy with which college students (N=296) were able to receive information under two conditions: Simultaneous Communication and Interpreted Communication. The results of the study led the authors to conclude that "...the use of simultaneous communication [is] preferable to interpreted communication for reception of information...."

Again there are limitations: (1) The stimulus material consisted of "two CID Everyday Sentence lists adapted for use at NTID...." Although there are a number of reasons for questioning the use of the CID Everyday Sentences in assessing receptive skills (Johnson and Cokely 1979), the most obvious difficulties are: (a) the assumption that high frequency words in written English are frequently used in spoken English and in manual or simultaneous communication or both; (b) the use of a list of unrelated sentences overlooks the important role of context in properly understanding any communication; (c) questionable proportions of sentence types represented in each list; and (d) performance measured by the number of "key words" correctly translated in each sentence. (2) The stimulus material was presented to the subjects using 3/4 inch color cassette videotapes. However, research has shown that deaf students "...can extract significantly more information from a lecture presented in a "live" mode than from visual motion media presentations of rear screen projection or television monitor." (Caccamise, Blaisdell & Meath–Lang 1977). Thus, the use of videotaped stimuli would tend to deflate student scores. It is not clear, however, whether scores would be deflated equally across simultaneous presen-tation and interpreted presentation. (3) The use of videotaped stimulus material also presents additional problems. In the case of the interpreted condition "...the speaker and interpreter stood about six inches apart with both appearing on the same screen." The proximity of interpreter to speaker seems quite extreme (Neumann–Solow 1981) and may have caused the interpreter to suppress certain behaviors that are often essential to effective interpreting (e.g. use of space and sign size variation). This would obviously affect the student's performance on the interpreted material. (4) No descriptive information is provided on the performance of the interpreter or on the performance of the simultaneous communicator. Thus, potential problems such as the distribution and frequency of fingerspelled words, rate of transmission, clustering of fingerspelled words and overall accuracy of the stimulus material are not discussed. However, a critique of the NTID Communication Performance Profile (which includes the two Everyday Sentence lists in this study) demonstrates that these problems can seriously affect student performance (Johnson & Cokely 1979). (5) Finally, the validity of the conclusions reached by the authors must be seriously questioned for the following reasons: (a) the study assumes that a student's ability to comprehend information from a lecture can be inferred from a student's ability to translate a list of unconnected English sentences. (b) The study assumes that lexical recall and recognition are adequate reflections of comprehension. (c) The study assumes that the amount of information received and understood by a student is equal to the number of "key words" the student translates correctly.

5. Jacobs (1977) designed this study "...to determine the amount of interpreted lecture information deaf students (N=29) were able to recall compared to the amount of lecture information recalled by hearing students through audition." The results indicated that "...interpreting is at least *84%* efficient in conveying college lecture information when compared to audition for hearing students ."

Limitations: (1) The stimulus material consisted of "...six short, interpreted lectures..." that prior to the experiment were "...simultaneously rehearsed by the lecturer and interpreter...." Knowing that the interpreter "rehearsed" the lectures, one could argue that, in fact, the stimulus was actually *not* interpreted but instead simultaneously delivered by two people—one using speech and one using sign alone. Furthermore, since the material was rehearsed, memorization behaviors may have influenced student performance. (2) Apparently only a single lecturer and a single interpreter were used throughout this study. Thus, the results of the study may not be generalized and may only hold for the two presenters. (3) No descriptive information is given on the performance of the lecturer or the "interpreter." It is possible that the results reflect interpreter error, distortion or deletion.

As the limitations indicate, representative studies in this area make use of unnatural stimulus material and fail to describe clearly what was being investigated. It seems appropriate, therefore, to question the research support for SC as the most effective means of communication in the classroom. Additionally, any meaningful study needs to avoid these limitations in order to yield valid and generalizable results.

A study of communication effectiveness

Three primary purposes for the pilot study undertaken were: (1) to determine the extent to which deaf college students (juniors and seniors) comprehend information in a college classroom setting presented in three ways: Simultaneous Communication, Sign Alone, and Interpretation; (2) to provide descriptive data on the note–taking performance of students in each of the three means of communication; (3) to provide descriptive data on the communicative performance of teachers in each of the three means of communication.

To obtain subjects, a letter was sent to all juniors and seniors at Gallaudet (N=347), asking if they would be willing to participate in the study. Positive replies were received from 119 students. Due to scheduling and time constraints, only 38 of the students were able to participate in the project. Each of the 38 students was asked to complete a background information sheet. There were 17 juniors and 21 seniors, 15 males and 23 females with an average age of 23 years. The students had been signing for an average of 15.5 years; seven of the students have deaf parents. The average hearing loss is 93.4 dB (right ear) and 93.1 dB (left ear); 47.4% consider themselves profoundly deaf, 36.8% consider themselves deaf, and 15.8%, hard of hearing. The students were asked to rate on a scale of 1 to 6 the extent to which they depend upon lip reading when communicating with hearing people at Gallaudet. The responses are presented in the following table:

Table 1 Subjects'self–rating of lipreading dependency.

Almost never		
	1	10.5%
	2	26.4%
	3	18.4%
	4	26.3%
	5	10.5%
Almost entirely	6	7.9%

Five members of the Gallaudet College undergraduate faculty also took part in the study. Each was asked to complete a background information sheet. The five, all male, ranged in age from 34 to 49 years old; average, 41. All five were hearing and had been teaching at Gallaudet for an average of 7.8 years, with a range of 4 to 14 years. Two of the five had been employed in non-teaching capacities (for 2 and 7 years respectively) before joining the teaching faculty. The five had been signing an average of 10.6 years, with a range of 4 to 20 years. None of them knew how to sign prior to employment at Gallaudet. At the time of the study, all held a Ph.D. (in one case, an equivalent terminal degree). All received passing grades on both the expressive and receptive portions of their most recent Simultaneous Communication evaluation (a routine for purposes of retention, promotion, etc.).

Two interpreters also participated in the study. Both were female and both held the Comprehensive Skills Certificate (CSC) from the Registry of Interpreters for the Deaf. The interpreters were obtained through the Gallaudet Interpreter Referral Service. There were only two conditions set for the selection of interpreters: first, each must hold a CSC certificate; second, each must be available to interpret on three specified dates.

Two undergraduate faculty members from the English Department, two from the Theater Arts Department and two from the Sociology/Social Work Department were asked to participate in the study. These academic areas were chosen because they are representative of the required (English) and elective (Theater Arts and Sociology/Social Work) courses students take at Gallaudet. Each pair of faculty members was asked to develop a class lecture (approximately 45 minutes in length) on a topic in their teaching area that they felt would be unfamiliar to juniors and seniors at Gallaudet. The topics they chose:

English—"Snow Imagery in Poetry"

Theater Arts—"Introduction to Style for a Theatrical Production"

Sociology/Social Work—"The Family as a Social Institution"

Each pair was then instructed to develop an agreed-upon list of 25 statements that represented the main ideas they wanted to convey about their topic (see appendix A). Using these statements, a 25 item multiple–choice cloze test was developed for each topic (see appendix B). A cloze format was chosen because it has been shown to take into account a number of variables that influence readability. A multiple–choice format was chosen for several reasons (McKee & Lang 1982): ease of scoring, expressed student preference, equal or greater reliability than true–false items, and the tendency of multiple–choice items to be more discriminating than true–false items. Each 25–item test was reviewed by the appropriate pair of teachers. This served two purposes: first, it allowed for modification of the test based on input from the teachers; second, it enabled the teachers to structure their lectures in such a way that they were able to "teach to the test." The original design of the study called for each student to attend three lectures—each lecture in a different content area and delivered by a different means of communication. This design is schematically represented in table 2.

Table 2. Initial design of study.

	English		Theater Arts		Sociology	
SC	TA G1	TB G4	TC G3	TD G6	TE G2	TF G5
Sign only	TA G2	TB G	TC G1	TD G4	TE G3	TF G6
Interpr'd	TA G3	TB G	TC G2	TD G5	TE G1	TF G4

Key: T, teacher   G, student group

Student groups were determined by random assignment within groups. The average number of students in each group was six. All lectures were held on Thursday and Friday afternoons over a four week period, with one week intervals between each lecture. Each lecture took place in a typical classroom on the campus of Gallaudet (Hall Memorial Building 307 & 315). Each lecture was videotaped using 3/4" color cassette equipment. Prior to their initial lecture, students were asked to complete a background questionnaire. They were also given notebooks and told that they might wish to take notes, because there would be a test at the end of each lecture. These notebooks were collected at the end of each lecture and returned before the start of the next lecture. The teachers were instructed to deliver their lecture on three successive weeks: once using SC, once just signing without voice (note that they were *not* told to use ASL nor to attempt to use ASL; simply to sign without talking), and once using an interpreter (i.e. they were simply to speak).

Results

Comprehension Tests. The results of the 25–item comprehension tests are presented in the following table. The mean score is presented for each content area by means of communication. Beside the mean score is the number of students in that cell.

Table 3. Mean scores for 25 item tests

	English	Theater arts	Sociology
SC	11.33 n= 9	14.14 n=14	13.75 n=4
Sign Alone	13.22 n= 9	13.54 n=11	13.16 n=6
Interpreted	13.73 n=15	11.72 n=11	14.12 n=8

The only statistically significant difference (at the 0.05 level) was for the ordering of the English lectures. Relative insensitivity of the testing instrumentation and the relatively small number of students in each lecture are two factors that directly influenced the statistical significance of the results. Therefore the discussion that follows should be read with this fact in mind.

An item analysis of the three 25 item tests revealed that a number of items in each test was statistically unreliable and nondiscriminating, (e.g. either all students in a group got the item correct or all students got it incorrect). Therefore any item shown to be unreliable and nondiscriminatory for any of the groups was eliminated from the analysis. This resulted in a 12 item test for English, a 13 item test for Theater Arts, and a 16 item test for Sociology. The following table presents the means for these revised tests. The number of students in each cell remains the same.

Table 3a. Mean scores for revised tests

	English	Theater arts	Sociology
SC	4.00	7.42	8.75
Sign Alone	6.56	8.45	8.50
Interpreted	6.47	6.27	10.13

Once again the differences were not shown to be statistically significant although there was some statistical support for the ordering reflected by these scores. A tentative indication of the effectiveness of the three means of communication can be obtained by examining the mean scores across content areas. This must be done cautiously, however, since the scores within cells are mean scores and a collapsed score across content areas will then be a mean of means. In addition, the Sociology/Social Work area is represented by a single teacher, which probably affects the scores for that area. The following ranking results from collapsing scores across content areas:

Table 4. Collapsed mean scores
(revised test) across content.

Sign alone	7.87
Interpreted	7.62
SC	6.72

If the Sociology/Social Work area is eliminated (for reasons noted above), the relative effectiveness ranking remains the same

Table 5. English & Theater Arts collapsed scores.

Sign alone	7.51
Interpreted	6.37
SC	5.71

Again, while this ranking is not borne out by tests of statistical significance, it does provide some indication of the relative effectiveness of the three means of communication. Interestingly enough, the same ordering is found if one uses the mean scores of the 25 item tests, although the means are much closer:

Table 6. Collapsed mean scores (25 item test) across content.

Sign alone	13.30
Interpreted	13.19
SC	13.07

B. Student note-taking. While a more extensive analysis of the student notebooks is planned, the following preliminary analysis can be offered. (1) Although quantity is rarely an indication of quality or utility, it is interesting to note that the average number of pages of notes taken by the students parallels the relative effectiveness ranking above. These averages are based on the notes of 16 students.

Table 7. Mean number of pages of notes per lecture.

SC	1.7 pages
Sign alone	3.3 pages
Interpreted	2.75 pages

One possible explanation for this is a heightened sensitivity on the part of the teachers when using Sign Alone or using an Interpreter; either would allow the students more opportunity to take notes. Another possible explanation is that increased concentration and attention is required under the SC conditions, which does not allow students the same note–taking opportunities as they have under the other two conditions. (2) On a qualitative level, preliminary analysis indicates differences in the form in which notes were taken under the three conditions. In general, notes taken under the Sign Alone and Interpreted conditions seem to resemble an outline or study–guide format; notes taken under the SC condition exhibit less order and structure. The following excerpts of three students" notes are reproduced verbatim:

Notes taken by **Student 1:**

SC   English   Topic, "Four poems"

   •snow

   •snow covered—suggests that one is lacking experience

•snow can be positive attitude

•seen that snow is really a realism

(1 page, total notes)

Sign Alone   Theater Arts   Topic, Style of play in theater:

1) Director - has final decision on style

2) Set Designer - responsible for design

3) Costume Designer - clothes design

4) Lighting Designer - light design

All four agree together to make a success

How to pick a style?

•technical to artist

•limit to or by technical

•same with theater, it can be limit in some ways

•E.G. in 1556, we can't copy their style actually   but get the feeling, emotion

(1 & 1/2 pages of 4 pages of notes)

Interpreted   Sociology   Topic, Definition of family
1) reproduction of new members of society
2) child care
3) socialization of children to the values, traditions & ranks
or positions of the society
4) intimacy & support for family members when tragic
occurred, family get together to support each other
                    (One page out of 2 1/2 pages of notes)

Notes taken by **Student 2:**

Interpreted   English   Topic, "Four poems"
•Nature influence human experience

•snow = lack of normal experience

•snow = absence of normal life

1) Poet's attitude: snow is good, friendly & positive or empty,
    cruel, show change

2) Diff. view of Amer. poet
    •mixed feeling
    •shows kind of emotion
                    (1 page out of 3 pages of notes)

SC   Theater Arts   Topic, Style of play in theater:
•1) Director   •different period

•2) Set Designer   •? style—unportant artist

•3) Costume Designer   •not copy same god—creative

•4) Lighting Designer   •not copy—in styles
                    (1 page of 2.5 pages of notes)

Sign Alone   Sociology   Topic, Definition of family
•Social functions of family
•1) reproduction of new members of society
•2) child care
•3) socialization of children
•4) intimacy and support

  extended family vs. nuclear family

(1 page of 3 pages of notes)

Notes taken by **Student 3:**

Sign Alone   English   Topic, "Four poems"
  •Poet shows human experience w/ nature in poetry
  •<u>Snow</u> = break of normal routine
  •absence of normal life
  •Poets attitudes differ   •sense of disappointment
  •"London Snow"
  •snow disrupted by businessmen
  •poet seems not to like it

(1 page of 3 pages of notes)

Interpreted   Theater Arts Topic, Style of play in theater:
  •<u>An Introduction to Theatrical Style</u>
  •<u>4 people involved in that</u> design

    1) director

    2) set designer

    3) costume designer

    <u>4) lighting designer</u>

  •Principles (Wolfflin)

    1) linear style vs. painterly style

    2) Depth of plane vs. recessional plane

(1 page of 3 pages of notes)

SC   *Sociology*   *Topic, Definition of family*
   family—"The" so changed the families
   variety of "the families"
   single family—4 things—1. important—female & male mate
      child is "illegitimate"
                              (1 page of 2 pages of notes)

While there are a number of possible explanations for the qualitative differences in these excerpts, it is apparent that under the Sign Alone and Interpreted conditions the students' notes better reflect the organization and structure of the lectures than do their notes under the SC condition. It does not appear that student's skill in taking notes is a factor since qualitative differences are apparent within the note-taking behavior of individual students. It also does not appear that content of the lecture is a significant factor. This is apparent when one realizes that in the excerpts presented above the three sets of notes that show the least organization, clarity and utility occur across content areas. In each case (Student 1 *English*, Student 2 *Theater Arts*, and Student 3 *Sociology*) the common denominator is that the lecture was delivered using Simultaneous Communication. Preliminary analysis indicates both quantitative and qualitative differences that suggest that students take more and better notes under the Sign Alone and Interpreting conditions than under the Simultaneous Communication condition.

C. *Teacher Performance*   Preliminary analysis of rate, vocalized pauses, and deletions in teacher performance shows the following results:

Rate: At least one research study (Baker 1980) has investigated comparative speaking and signing rates of transmission of hearing people in *conversational discourse* when using SC:

Table 8. Conversation rates for hearing people (Baker 1980).

Sign alone/PSE	SC		Speech alone
signs/minute	*s/min*	*w/min*	*w/min*
103	93	162	216

These rates indicate a 25% decrease in speaking rate when using SC and a 10% decrease in signing rate—in conversational settings. Given that ethnographic research has shown that a number of factors (e.g. setting, purpose, participants) can affect discourse, and given that a classroom lecture is generally considered more formal than conversational discourse, one would expect a difference in transmission rates. If there is validity to the claim that rate is affected when a person has to think about the content of a message as well as think about how to encode it simultaneously (Baker 1980), then one would expect a decreased transmission rate under the SC condition in the classroom.

Tapes of four of the five teachers in this study were analyzed for rate, as shown in Table 9. The value for each teacher is the average rate of a 3 minute sample taken for that teacher under each condition. For the 3-minute sample, the first minute of continuous discourse was taken 10 minutes into the lecture, the second minute was taken 15 minutes into the lecture, and the final minute 20 minutes into the lecture.

Table 9. Classroom lecture rates.

	Sign only *s/min*	SC (signs) *s/min*	SC (voice) *w/min*	Interpreted *w/min*
Tchr 1*	66.6	61.3	110.6	136.3
Tchr 2*	78.0	62.6	109.3	116.3
Tchr 3^	71.3	62.3	107.0	115 .0
Tchr 4^	76.3	66.0	117.3	143.6
Average	73.1	63.1	111.1	127.8

Key: *, Theater Arts; ^, English

These results show that when using SC in a lecture situation teachers slow down their signing rate by 13.7% and slow down their speaking rate by 13.0%. The differences between decreased rates of transmission when using SC in a conversational setting (decrease of 25% wpm and 10% spm) and in a classroom lecture setting (decrease of 13.0% wpm and 13.7% spm) can, in part, be attributed to the relative formality of the classroom setting.

It is also possible that the decreased speaking rate in the classroom situation in this study is influenced by the presence of an interpreter. That is, the teacher"s normal speaking rate may be slowed down to accommodate the interpreter. This decrease is in addition to the rate decrease attributable to the setting. The classroom setting, then, seems to result in a decreased rate of transmission in all conditions as can be seen from the following table:

Table 10. Comparison of conversational and classroom rates

	Sign alone *s/min*	SC (signs) *s/min*	SC (wds) *w/min*	Interpret'd *w/min*
Convers'n	103.0	93.0	162.0	216.0
Classroom	73.1	63.1	111.1	127.8

Of course these data must be interpreted cautiously since the rates are not taken from the same individuals. Nonetheless, it does seem apparent that the classroom setting brings a decreased rate of transmission. Additionally, the rate count given here does not address the issue of propositional rate; i.e. it may be possible that a given proposition or meaning can be expressed in fewer signs than words thus accounting for some of the rate differences given in this section.

Vocalized pauses. The videotaped data samples described above also showed that teachers use the word "okay" and the corresponding fingerspelled loan sign #OK[1] differently under SC conditions from

---

[1] ASL sign derived from fingerspelling of 'O-K' (Battison 1978: 123f)

the way that they use the loan sign #OK under Sign-Alone conditions. More specifically the uses of #OK and "okay"/.#OK appear to have different functions under SC conditions and Sign-Alone conditions. Under SC conditions, the word "okay" seems to function primarily as a self-reassurance device. That is, the word is used by teachers speaking and signing simultaneously as a means of self-feedback. It seems to carry a meaning such as "Whew! I got through that, now on to the next idea. . ." That the word has some such function can be seen by comparing the frequency of the word "okay" with the frequency of the word plus the sign ("okay"/#OK) and the frequency of the sign #OK. Note that frequencies are taken from the SC samples described above.

Table 11. Frequencies of #OK & "okay", SC condition only.

	Spoken 'okay'	SC #OK / 'okay	Signed #OK
Teacher 1	6	2	0
Teacher 2	12	1	0
Teacher 3	18	8	0
Teacher 4	10	1	0
Totals	46	12	0
Averages	11.5	3	

Thus, although teachers used the word "okay" an average of 11.5 times in three minutes, it was signed an average of only 3 times. Further, the sign #OK was not used alone. Thus, 74% of the time that the word "okay" is used it is not directed at the students. Of those instances when "okay" and #OK do occur together (N=12) only 2 are actual questions (i.e. "You understand?") as evidenced by intonation contour, non-manual behaviors, eye gaze, and pausing, behaviors. Thus only 16.6% of the simultaneous use of "okay" and #OK are questions and only 4.3% of the instances of " okay " are questions.

Table 12. Frequency of #OK under Sign-Alone condition.

	#OK occurrenc	#OK as question
Teacher 1	2	2
Teacher 2	5	3
Teacher 3	7	5
Teacher 4	2	1
Totals	16	11
Averages	4	2.8

While simultaneously produced "okay"/#OK functions as a question 16.6% of the time under SC, #OK functions as a question 68.9% of the time under Sign Alone. The fact that #OK occurs less frequently under Sign Alone than "okay" occurs under SC suggests that teachers may have less need of a self-reassurance device under Sign-Alone conditions than under SC conditions. Another indication of this is that no instances of "okay" were found under the Interpreted condition.

Deletions. Previous research (Baker 1980) has shown that under SC conditions in a conversational setting, deletions do occur that seem to be attributable to rate of transmission differences. At a conversational rate of 162 wpm and 93 spm (a rate difference of 69), there are signed omissions that directly, affect the meaning of sentences. These omissions are not simply omissions of grammatical forms, but are omissions of content signs that render the signed portions of SC messages confusing or different from the meaning of the spoken portions. It seems highly likely, then, that given lecture rates of 63.1 spm and 111.1 wpm (a rate difference of 48), omissions will also occur. The type, frequency and significance of such omissions await further analysis.

Conclusion

The results of this pilot study run counter to the findings of previous research in this area. These results can be summarized as follows:

A. Student comprehension tests, though not statistically significant, show Sign Alone as the most effective means of conveying information in the college, classroom and SC the least effective;

B. Students" note-taking was greater in quantity and better in quality under the Sign.Alone and Interpretation conditions;

C Teacher"s communicative performance with SC was slower and showed less communicative confidence.

While there are admitted limitations to this pilot study (most notably the need for more sensitive comprehension tests); nonetheless, the results all seem to indicate that SC may not be the most effective means of classroom communication. Consider the following facts:

1. The comprehension tests ranked Sign Alone above Interpreted, which ranked above SC;
2. A quantitative analysis of student notes resulted in identical ranking: Sign Alone, Interpreted, SC ;
3. The quality and utility of student notes taken across all three content areas under Sign Alone and Interpreted conditions were superior to notes taken when presentation was in SC;
4 Higher transmission rates were found for Sign Alone and Interpreted conditions than for SC;
5. A higher incidence of "vocalized pauses" was found under the SC condition than for the Sign Alone or Interpreted condition.

One implication of these facts is that for efficiency in com-municating information in the college classroom, it may be preferable for the teacher to use sign without speaking or to use an interpreter. Another implication is that when hearing teachers use sign without speaking, even though the signing is still more like English than it is like ASL, the organization and structure of their lectures is more readily discernable to students. Finally, it appears that teachers show a higher degree of confidence in their ability to sign without speaking than in their ability to use SC. The results of this pilot study provide additional qualitative and quantitative support for those who argue that the demands of signing and speaking at the same time directly affect the quality of communication in the classroom. Although further investigation of student comprehension is needed, the results of this pilot study indicate that classroom communication using Simultaneous Communication is less advantageous than has been previously argued. Even without statistically significant differences in comprehension tests, the effects of using SC in the classroom on teacher performance and on student note-taking ability cannot be dismissed lightly. The utility of any means of communication that negatively affects the teacher"s ability to convey information and, at the same time, the student"s ability to record that information for later review must be seriously questioned.

Appendix A.

Summary statements for each lecture
(to compare with student notes):

Snow Imagery in Poetry • Poems used in the lecture:

    LS   "London Snow" by Robert Bridges
    SM   "The Snow Man" by Wallace Stevens
    DP   "Desert Places" by Robert Frost
    SA   "Snowfall in the Afternoon" by Robert Bly

[Copies of the poems were distributed at the beginning of each lecture; transparencies (initials below) of the poems will be used during the lectures.]

1. Poets often use things from nature to talk about human experiences .
2. Snow is often used by poets to picture the absence of a normal life experience.
3. In the past, the absence of normal life experience was usually good, but now poets see it as more friohtening.
4. LS. The snow in the poem is "friendly" because it allows for a break in the daily routine.
5. LS. The "sombre men" going to work pause for a moment and enjoy the snow but then resume their daily routine and the "charm" of the snow is broken.
6. LS. The poet enjoys how quiet London is with the snow; there is a sense of relief about the "break" and a sense of anger that the businessmen start the routine going again.
7. SM. Wallace Stevens feels that most people don"t like winter or snow, but he says that the "bareness" of winter actually makes it easier to understand what the universe is like.
8. SM. If you want to understand the world, Stevens says, you have to ignore your personal discomfort and look at nature objectively. In this way, a person can look at the world the way it really is, "beholding nothing that is not there."
9. SM. So, in this poem, snow is seen as both positive and negative: it symbolizes an absence of human feeling but at the same time that absence allows for a clearer perception of reality.

10. DP. "Desert" in this poem means "deserted," "without people."
11. DP. Robert Frost has a similar feeling to Wallace Stevens in "The Snow Man" in that he also feels like "nothing" ("I am too absent-spirited to count").
12. DP. The snow covers up the signs of human work—the cleared field and the stubble from last summer"s crop—and makes the scene seem non-human.
13. DP. The snow in this poem seems to represent a way of nature reclaiming its own: it shows the poet that nature is basically alien and empty (it has "nothing to express").
14. DP. The poet compares the snowed-over field to the empty spaces between stars and he concludes that those spaces are no more empty or scary than those right here on earth.
15. SA. The snow makes a cover or "roof" on the spaces in the grass and the poet notices that these "little houses" are dark.
16. SA. Bly feels that the darkness in the grass is always there and the snow shows us that.
17. SA. Bly is like Frost and Stevens because he also feels that snow makes it possible for us to see the true reality of the universe.
18. SA. Bly, like Bridges and Frost, portrays snow gradually covering up the familiar sights outside his house and therefore changing the way he sees the world .
19. SA. The poet feels that snow obliterates the familiar and makes the world seem strange, but he also seems to see things he doesn"t norrnally see.
20. SA. For Bly, being "blind" is not necessarily a bad thing because he believes we can see more of the true world if we look inward.
21. In all of the poems, snow represents a way of covering up something human.
22. Snow symbolizes a suspension of normal life.
23. Poets writing about snow often show mixed feelings, describing snow as almost scary because it leads us to see the world in a different way.
24. In the poems we discussed, snow represents altered perception, a covering up of human emotion.
25. The three American poets, Stevens, Frost and Bly, write poems that sound like the mood they describe: the poems

are bare and simple, and don"t seem to have much feeling in them.

Introduction to Style for a Theatrical Production

1. The style of a theatrical production is the result of various complicated factors.
2. In theater design, as in other kinds of art, the final product in no way reproduces the reality of a particular historical period.
3. Art is limited, controlled, and defined by the technical experience of the artist.
4. Ideally, a production should be designed to illuminate the structure and plan of the play.
5. When the director and designer discuss the design for a play, they should stress making the inner structure of the play become visual.
6. In *Principles of Art History*, Heinrich Wolfflin described five ways to explain the differences in historical periods.
7. A linear style emphasizes clear outlines and obvious details.
8. A painterly style blurs the edges, merges objects, and gives a shifting appearance to objects.
9. In depth of plane style, space is organized as a series of receding planes.
10. In recessional depth style, the sense of plane is broken and visual space goes back in depth on diagonal lines.
11. In a closed composition, objects are rigidly framed and enclosed, while in open compositions they are merged with outside space.
12. Another way to discuss style is to look at individual details that keep their identity while fitting into the whole picture, as opposed to a style where the details and individual elements cannot be distinguished.
13. The difference between relative clarity and absolute clarity involves how light is used.
14. The history of visual arts can be seen as an ongoing pendulum shift from abstraction to reality, from the irrational to the rational, and back again.

15. Expressionism, impressionism, surrealism, symbolism, naturalism, and realism can be grouped in relation to classical or romantic styles.
16. A theater designer must always make a choice between using visual material to illuminate a historical period directly, or to comment on the period and illuminate it subtly.
17. A stylized production stresses line, texture, and color instead of visual reality.
18. The theatrical designer is an interpreter of another man"s artistic product.
19. Theatrical design should be beautiful in its own way as a modern design, and yet keep forms from the past in which the particular play developed.
20. Successful theater design combines all that can be learned about a play and its background with visual sources and design concepts of today.
21. The recreation of the past or present in theatrical design is impossible.
22. Classical style describes a work that stresses order, structure, logic, and simplicity.
23. Romantic style describes a work that is rich in emotion, sensuous appeal, and complex action.
24. All that is ever presented on stage is a personal interpretation of visual reality.
25. Art filters life.

The Family as a Social Institution

1. In viewing the family as a social institution, the focus is not on a specific family style, but on elements common to all forms families may take.
2. The social functions that are carried out by families throughout the world are: 1. reproduction of new members of the society; 2. child care; 3. socialization of children to the values, traditions, and ranks or positions of the society; 4. intimacy and support for family members.
3. Families are both biological and social units.
4. At least in the United States, it is still generally true that a child conceived out of wedlock, is considered "illegitimate" if

no male acknowledges the child as his or no male assumes responsibility for the child.

5. Regardless of the variations among accepted norms, every society in the world controls biological parenthood. (Biological sex drives are always harnessed in some way— taboos, etc.)

6. Having a baby may be a biological fact, but creating a family is clearly a social fact.

7. Evidence indicates a close connection between the organizational structure of the family and specific patterns of subsistence. (Agricultural and fishing societies encourage large families, hunting and gathering societies, small families.)

8. Prior to the Industrial Revolution, the American economy was predominately agricultural and family life was organized around agricultural production.

9. The most common type of family during the preindustrial era was the extended family.

10. Extended families generally consist of a married couple, their children, and a number of other relatives, all of whom share a common domicile.

11. In order to prosper in farming, it was useful for a man to have a robust and industrious wife and many children to help with the work.

12. A paramount belief within the extended family structure was the idea that the individual was always secondary to the welfare of the family unit. (For example, in preindustrial America, if a husband and wife were trying to decide whether their eldest son should marry a particular woman, his individual preferences would be less important in the decision than the perceived welfare of the family as a unit.)

13. Social roles in the extended family were relatively clear-cut and well defined.

14. Geographic mobility was considered undesirable and suspicious for preindustrial families.

15. The "extended" structure of the preindustrial family was consistent with the economic and social demands of that period.

16. As industrialization progressed in the United States, the economic functions of the extended family steadily declined.

17. In industrialized America, the family became a more consumption-oriented unit, rather than a production unit.

18. The nuclear family emerged with the rise of industrialization.
19. The nuclear family usually consisted of a husband, wife, and their immediate children.
20. With the nuclear family, marriage became more a matter of personal choice than of economic necessity.
21. With the rise of industrialization, children were less likely to be economic assets and more often were liabilities as compared with preindustrial America.
22. With the nuclear family, the belief that the individual was always secondary to the welfare of the family unit began to be replaced by the belief that the desires of the individual take precedence over the needs of the family.
23. Changes brought about by industrialization had some dramatic effects on the role structure of the family.
24. Romantic love plays an important role in nuclear families.
25. As a basis of marriage, romantic love has its limitations.

Appendix B.

Samples of multiple-choice test items.

(Circle the letter that you feel best fits in the blank)

ENGLISH

1. Poets often use _____ to talk about human experiences.

a. words that sound the same   b. snow

c. strange poems   d. things from nature

e. words that they invent

•

4. London Snow: The snow in the poem is _____ because it allows for a break in the daily routine.

a. "scary"   b. "deep"

c. "hateful"   d. "awful"

d. "friendly"

•

21. In all of the poems, snow represents a way of _____ .

a. describing end of the world

b. covering something human

c. forgetting unpleasant memories

d. showing the world is cold

e. covering up nature

THEATER ARTS

2. The style of a theatrical production is the result of _____ .

a. always reproduces   b. is an exact copy of

c. totally ignores   d. in no way expresses

e. is a bad copy of

•

5. When the director and designer discuss the design for a play they should stress making _____ the play become visual.

a. the action in   b. the cast of

c. the scenery in   d. the inner structure of

e. the characters in

•

10. In recessional depth style, the sense of the plane is broken and visual space goes back in depth _____ .

a. on diagonal lines   b. in circles

c. on crooked lines   d. on straight lines

e. to the end of the stage

REFERENCES

Baker, C.
>1981 How does SC fit into a bilingual approach to
>education? In *Proceedings of NSSLRT II*, Silver
>Spring, MD: National Association of the Deaf.

Caccamise, F. & R. Blaisdell
>1977 Reception of sentences under oral-manual, interpreted
>& simultaneous test conditions, *American Annals of the
>Deaf* 122, 414-421.

Caccamise, F., R. Blaisdell & B. Meath-Lang
>1977 Hearing impaired persons" simultaneous reception of
>information under live & two visual motion media
>conditions, *American Annals of the Deaf* 122, 339-343

Chafe, W. (Ed.)
>1980 *The Pear Stories*. 1977. Norwood, NJ: Ablex Publ. Co.

Cokely, D.
>1979 The Simultaneous Method of Communication. In *Pre-
>College Programs: Guidelines for Manual
>Communication*. Washington: Pre-College Programs,
>Gallaudet College.

Freedle, R. (Ed.)
>1979 *New Directions in Discourse Processing*. Norwood,
>NJ: Ablex.

Jacobs, L.
>1977 The efficiency of interpreting input for processing
>lecture information by deaf college students, *Journal of
>Rehabilitation of the Deaf* 2, 10-15.

[Johnson, R. & D. Cokely
>1979 Critical Assessment of the NTID Communication
>Performance Profile: Manual & Simultaneous Reception
>Tests (unpublished manuscript).]

Klopping, H.

1972 Language understanding of deaf students under three auditory–visual stimulus conditions, *American Annals of the Deaf* 117, 389-396.

Kluwin, T.

1981 A rationale for modifying classroom signing systems, *Sign Language Studies* 31, 179-187.

McKee, B. & H. Lang

1982 A Comparison of deaf students" performance on true-false & multiple-choice items, *American Annals of the Deaf* 127, 49-54.

Marmor, G. & L. Petitto

1979 Simultaneous communication in the classroom: How grammatical is it? *Sign Language Studies* 23, 99-136.

Neumann-Solow, S.

1981 *Sign Language Interpreting: A Basic Resource Book.* Silver Spring, MD: National Association of the Deaf.

Newell, W.

1978 A study of the ability of day-class deaf adolescents to comprehend factual information using four communication modalities, *American Annals of the Deaf* 123, 558-562.

White, A. & V. Stevenson

1975 The effects of total communication, manual communication, oral communication & reading on the learning of factual information in residential school deaf children, *American Annals of the Deaf* 120, 48-57.